The Journeying Self

The Journeying Self

The Gospel of Mark
Through a Jungian Perspective

Diarmuid McGann

PAULIST PRESS
New York/Ramsey

Library of Congress Catalog Card Number: 84-61492

ISBN: 0-8091-2662-1

Published by Paulist Press
997 Macarthur Boulevard
Mahwah, New Jersey 07430

Printed and bound in the United States of America

Contents

v

Contents

Preface

I have been very fortunate during the course of my lifetime so far to have had many excellent teachers who have passed on to me the wisdom they have accrued over a lifetime. While this book is the result of all of them it is in particular my own effort to draw the different strands of four main teachers together in my own way.

My first teacher was my family of origin, my parents, three brothers and a sister. In particular from my father I learned a love for poetry and for the earth. He was an extroverted fun-loving man who would attempt to gather people together to celebrate life, in music, in song, and in poetry. Always at center stage he was at his best when people were enjoying themselves. Dad died in my arms with our family gathered around him in prayer during the year I was writing the final chapters of this book. Living with an extrovert is not always the easiest of tasks. He takes the limelight, steals the show; life happens around him. He is always where the action is, where the life is flowing. My mother is more on the introverted side. She loves music, flowers, gardening. She is the even, attentive, vigilant presence that nourishes and strengthens the family. From her I learned

1

much about suffering. As a young woman she broke her neck in a car crash. She and dad raised five children, she stood by my older brother in his very difficult days, and was there for my sister when she was hospitalized for a few years. Mom knew suffering and how to draw strength from some source in the middle of it to keep us going. Even now in old age, with blindness upon her, she is a woman of faith and love.

My brothers and my sister were also very important in my formation. My older brother whom I tried to understand but who was always different from me first excited my attention to the inner world. My twin brother with whom I competed, at times fiercely even if he didn't know it, whom I admired and was jealous of all at once, and my younger brother so like my father in laughter and song and yet so much his own man achieving greatness and admiration on the fields of play and sport—both taught me something of discipline, challenge and determination. My sister was a great help to me in my growing years. With her I felt I could share the secrets and uncertainties of my existence. She was, and is to me, a great receiver of hurting people and she heals them with her caring. Very briefly, and totally inadequate to express the reality of what I experienced, that is my family of origin, and my first teacher.

My second great teacher came when I entered the major seminary in Carlow. He was a tall, thin man, seemingly very different from me. His eyes lit up however when he moved among the flowers and trees and bushes. He was a very gentle man, a lover of nature and of all things growing. More than anything else Fr. P.J. Brophy seemed to love Scripture. The way he spoke of it, listened to it, prayed it, and celebrated it said something to me of its position and presence in his life. In all honesty I must say I learned very little of Scripture from him because I wasn't that interested in "his subject matter" at that time. Moses, Isaiah and the other characters of Scripture seemed strange to me. Nevertheless his love for Scripture came across, and that love somehow reached down inside me and was activated slowly as my life evolved.

The third great teacher of my life I never met in person, only through his writings. He had a profound effect upon my life and indeed changed its direction. I came across his writings shortly after an illness that had kept me away from parish duties for a few months. The minute I read his work I could feel the excitement in me. I knew I was reading someone who understood me, even though I didn't understand him at all. Teilhard de Chardin's book *The Hymn of the Universe* jumped at me. Gradually I read all of his works. Much of what he wrote I was not equipped to comprehend but he seemed, especially in *The Hymn*, and in *The Divine Milieu*, to put words on things and experiences that made sense to me. Through him I came to understand life as growth, as process, as change. I came to touch and feel the hope of a personalizing goal that was drawing man forward. I came to understand more about the unity of the universe and the new story of humanity, the vision of not only cosmogenesis but Christogenesis.

The last teacher I will mention is again a group of people. These were my professors and fellow students in psychology at Iona College in New York. They encouraged me to pursue my interest in psychology. Gradually they helped me to understand something about the human person. They taught me to be more attentive to me, to the messages I was getting from my feelings, etc. They helped me to respect and reverence the confusion and differences of others and to stand before the mystery of another person. When a few years ago I first had the idea for this book and shared it with some of them, they encouraged me to go ahead, to risk it in the knowledge that if something is worth doing it's worth doing badly. Things don't have to be perfect, and everything a man's life might say cannot be said before it's over.

These were a few of my teachers. My task is to bring to synthesis in me what I have learned from them. At times the pieces fit. Many times they don't. T.S. Eliot expresses this in his poem "Hints and Guesses."[1] He speaks of the "point of intersection of the timeless/ with time." This dimension of awareness is the awareness and activity of the saint "something given/ and taken in a lifetime's death in love." For the rest of us who are not saints there is "only the unattended moment/ the moment in and out of time." This is a moment when you see for a second and then the vision is gone. It's a moment in which there are "hints and guesses/ hints followed by guesses and the rest/ is prayer, etc." This book is for me my first attempt at putting the hints and guesses together.

I am aware from the beginning that this meditation will rekindle the question of the relationship between psychology and religion. Some would see that there can never be a meeting between these two disciplines. Some will claim that psychology is a science while theology is a philosophical system. Others will claim that both study the human person in his value system, interrelationships, etc. In a recent work John D. Carter and Bruce Narramore[2] have indicated that in the "brief one-hundred year history of psychology there have been numerous attempts to relate the facts and theories of psychology to the affirmations of theology and that these attempts run the gamut from outright rejection of integrating two such separate disciplines to some very sophisticated attempts to find common ground and integrable concepts in the statements of psychologists and theologians." They suggest that there are four general approaches to models of integration: the "against" model (these are totally opposed to any integration at all), the "of" model (who hold there is a great deal of common ground between the two), the "parallels" model (who see that both have their rightful place but rarely integrate), and the "integrates" model (who hold that the two can mesh together since the truth is one and anything that is true in psychology cannot contradict the truth that is in Jesus).

My purpose is not to resolve any of these issues, although I am familiar with their existence as serious questions within both the psychological and theological field.[3] My purpose in writing this book is to bring the quiltwork, the patchwork of my experiences together. I write then not to give a hypothetical answer to the problem of theology and psychology but to bring the story of my life and the story of the Gospel into greater harmony.

Not only have I been fortunate to have had great teachers in my life, but I also have been privileged to experience the warm support of many friends. Their presence in my life is reflected constantly in this book and I express my gratitude to them. In particular I must single out two very special friends: Rev. Peter Mann whose encouraging conversations, challenging confrontations, and insightful observations have not only been of inestimable help to me personally but have also helped to shape this work; and Ms Darcy Upton who tirelessly and patiently gave herself to the very difficult task of translating my penmanship into readable English and typing this manuscript in its numerous drafts.

Chapter 1
Beginning

The Markan Gospel has been a treasure store for the Christian community since its earliest days. It has, in the nearly two thousand years of its existence, enjoyed great favor at times among biblical scholars, and at other times it seems to have been thought of as relatively insignificant.[1] During these periods it was Matthew's and Luke's Gospels that drew all the attention. In recent years Mark seems to have become once again a focus for the attention of scholars. The reasons for this are many and are well documented elsewhere. It is sufficient to indicate here that the history of Jesus as presented in the Gospel is the history of the Markan author putting together elements of a personal story, that of Jesus, with elements of a collective memory. The resulting Gospel is at once a story of Jesus, a story of the community or Church of Mark's time, and it is also a story of the individual disciple. Mark is conveying what discipleship means, and his Gospel reflects his viewpoint. It is different in nuance and emphasis from the other Gospels. Matthew, Luke and John, who followed, used somewhat the same stories, traditions, memories, etc., and arranged

7

them with their own emphasis so as to reflect their particular theological vision. Mark's Gospel is the story of Jesus
the model confessor in the midst of suffering, the believer
in life in the midst of conflict, the one who enters darkness
and death, the unknown and the hidden, and brings forth
life and meaning.

One can approach this Gospel in many ways as history
demonstrates. We have had the attempt of the "tendencies
critics" to delineate the theological aims of the Gospel, and
the efforts of "source criticism" to inform us on what
sources were used in constructing the Gospels. Later on the
"form critics" approached the Gospel to discover what
influences were at work in different parables, etc., and the
life situation in which this teaching emerged. Then the
"redaction critics" examined the Gospel to see if they could
determine what changes the later author made on the original stories by way of editing. In recent years we have a new
group of biblical scholars who are studying the Gospel from
the literary and structural point of view. Among these are
Werner Kelber,[2] Donald Michie and David Rhoads.[3] They
ask us to approach the Gospel as a unit, as a single whole,
to "observe the characters and the interplay among them,
to watch for the author's clues regarding the plot, to discern
the plot development, to identify scenes of crisis and recognition, and to view the story's resolution in the light of
its antecedent logic."[4]

I have been deeply influenced by reading the work of
these men, particularly Werner Kelber. I have found his
writing stimulating and challenging, and it underlies much
of the biblical approach in this work. I recognize the caution
expressed by Rhoads and Michie that "in narrative study
we cannot legitimately use the other Gospel stories to fill
out, or to fill in some unclear passage in Mark's story."[5]
Nevertheless I have chosen at times to ignore this caution

in the interest of pursuing my own particular viewpoint. I believe that Scripture is essential to understanding who we are as a people, and who I am as a person and as an individual. What, I began to wonder some years ago, would happen if the Gospels were seen not only as a story of Jesus, but as a story of me, of who I am and who I am becoming? What if the story of the Scripture is my story in and through the story of Jesus? What if the universe itself is coming to birth in and through that story? These questions on both the individual and the cosmic level began to intrigue me. I have chosen to explore in this work the implication and possibilities of that question against the background of the particular psychological viewpoint espoused in the writings of Carl Gustav Jung.[6]

Jung along with Freud and others acknowledges that the conscious life is only the tip of the iceberg. A human also has an unconscious, and for Jung this has two aspects. This makes for a three-layer system that is constantly interacting. Acknowledging that we are grossly oversimplifying Jung, we can say that the personal unconscious consists of our own story, our own lived conscious history which has in part been repressed. All of us have had to repress some of our memories, feelings, experiences which we have known. For many different reasons these have left the conscious mind. The collective unconscious on the other hand belongs to the history of mankind. We all carry within us the imprint of evolution's history not only physically but psychically. These are the results of heredity and evolution. They reflect the typical experiences of man and so provide a pattern of meaning for the person. They give us information of the way forward if we learn to read them. For Jung the archetype of wholeness is the self which lies at the center and the periphery of the personality at the same time. It is a goal never reached yet always sought. It is the

goal of living. For Jung a person is both known and
unknown, conscious and unconscious, an ego and a self;
and individuation, his name for growing into wholeness
consists in developing the axis between the two.[7]

The word self has many different uses. At times it
refers to my immediate conscious awareness of who I am.
Sometimes it refers to the hidden repressed me, the personal unconscious. Jung speaks of the self, and by it he
means the objective psyche. I have used the term in all of
these ways but I also include it to speak of that ineffable
self that man is at the core of his being where he is made
in the image and likeness of God. Generally it is this last
meaning which I have in mind when I speak of the story of
self.

There is at the heart of Jungian psychology a tension
between opposites and a call to wholeness. Whatever differences there are between Jungian psychology and the
Gospel, there is at least this same kind of energy tension at
the heart of the Gospel. The Kingdom, as Mark sees it, is
already among you and yet there is a not-yet quality to it.
Our lives flow from the interplay between these two poles.
Yes Jesus has come, yes the Kingdom is here, and yet we
readers are invited to grow and to leave behind our old way
of life. We are invited on the journey of Jesus. Our lives thus
flow from an interplay of meaning that is at once both created by us and revealed by God in Christ. The story of the
direction, development, and meaning of life unfolds in
stages in and through the unfolding of Jesus in the Scriptures. This book therefore is an attempt to relate the movement and structure of the Markan Gospel to the inner
human journey of the person through the analytic psychology of Jung, and perhaps at some later date to see it in terms
of the cosmic journey itself.

Susan Muto[8] has indicated the need for a person who hopes to approach a text meditatively, to "slow down," to "step aside" from partial truths, to "be with the text," ruminating upon it and letting it come alive within us. The danger is that we will fall into old patterns by trying to grasp it scientifically or by overpowering and dominating the text. We have tried to let our reading of the Markan Gospel be meditative. It has been the catalyst for my prayer and preaching for a long time now. I have read and reread the stories until gradually they began to read me, to attack my way of seeing life and reality. Gradually they have revealed within me the many dimensions of myself, opening me at times painfully to the Pharisees and scribes, etc., within, at times joyfully to the gifts of my life, and even at times to the Christ center, the original word of God placed at the center of my life. The symbols of the story then awaken my life at different levels and open me with hints and guesses, with discipline and prayer to the beauty ever ancient, ever new, as it reveals itself in my life.

Chapter 2
Good News

Mark begins his Gospel with the announcement "The beginning of the Gospel of Jesus Christ the Son of God" (1:1). This is the title and the beginning of the book. It is also a synopsis of the whole book. Edward Schillebeeckx has shown how the title "embraces the whole book. . . . The Gospel has its beginning in the appearance of the advent messenger, the Baptist, along with the subsequent ministry of Jesus of Nazareth, his message about the imminent rule of God, his travelling here and there doing good, his intercourse with tax collectors and sinners, his favorable stories, but all this meets with resistance and in the end leads to suffering and death, and still above and beyond comes God's message: This man is risen. With that the Gospel of Mark ends; all that is the beginning of the glad tidings of Jesus Christ."[1] The Gospel therefore must be seen and appreciated in its totality, and it is only then that it is seen as good news. It is also only then that it can be seen as beginning. The person too must be seen in totality and not in piecemeal fashion. Only then is life seen as good news

12

and as beginning. It is this Gospel that Mark now opens for our consideration.

It begins by presenting Jesus, but the very manner in which he does this is itself interesting. Unlike Matthew and Luke who present us with flowing genealogical trees, Mark's Christ is presented without antecedents. There is no record of his parental lineage, no account of the awesome virgin birth, no flights to faraway countries. Mark's curiosity is not aroused by biographical details. It is Jesus himself who seems to hold his attention. From the very beginning, as Kelber comments, "Jesus is the man who came from Nazareth of Galilee. From the outset Jesus is coming in motion from place to place."[2] In the Gospel everybody else stands before this movement. Some are struck by amazement, others by awe and wonder, others are shocked and thrown in confusion. Through all of this Jesus continues to emerge and move into the depth of things, into the reality of life. This is what appears to capture Mark's attention.

As Jesus moves forward into the depths he conveys his conviction that even though people think that they exist as independents, as worlds unto themselves alone, there is nevertheless an underlying unity. They have come from a deeper source and they exist in relation to it. Jesus is the visible manifestation of that source and their relationship to him indicates their relationship to God, the ultimate ground of being. Everyone in the Gospel, even Jesus himself, stands before this mystery. The Gospel characters stand questioning, wondering, challenging and discovering something of this mystery of who he is.[3] This is, as I understand it, the best meaning of what Markan scholars call the "messianic secret."

Seen as a story of self what is this opening saying to us? Is it revelatory for the meditator? I gaze upon this Gospel, this good news, recognizing that now I stand before my life at a point somewhere between birth and death. I begin to understand that the self that I am is from the beginning a mystery, and that my whole life from birth to death is only a beginning. I recognize the truth of what Eliot said, that "the end of all our journeys will be to return to the place from which we started and know it for the first time."[3] The self that I am emerges out of infinity, but it is related to it and is indeed in some way a manifestation of it. I am the personalizing face of a personal infinity. I have antecedents but they are only of relative importance. Everything else within me, behind me, and ahead of me stands before the mystery that I am. This is the wonder of my existence. I am more than a something that is determined by biological forces, instincts, or drives. I am a self even before the coming of consciousness.

In the opening segments of the Gospel Jesus is baptized in the Jordan by John the Baptist. He comes to John willing to be judged, not presuming to pass judgment on himself. John is a powerful influence on Jesus and in many ways acts as a role model for him.[4] The great changes in Jesus' life center on his contact with John the Baptist.[5] Indeed what happens at this point is that Jesus, "who is ready to take his place among sinners, receives and experiences unconditional acceptance from God. . . . He came ready to receive condemnation for his past and received instead unconditional acceptance."[6]

In the baptismal scene clustered around Christ are a concentric grouping of symbols. They are all attempting to answer the question: Who is he? In the Markan account it is only Jesus himself who sees and hears the great happenings. It is presented as an event that occurs between Jesus and the Father. There are five elements to the theophany or vision: 1. Coming out of the water. 2. Heavens above open.

3. Spirit comes like a dove. 4. Voice speaks: "You are my beloved Son." 5. Jesus alone sees the vision. These five symbols seek to mediate the meaning of the event. The fact that there are five symbols is itself interesting since five is frequently symbolic of health and love, "of the quintessence acting on matter."[7] The symbols constitute both memory and recall on the one hand and they are invitation and summons on the other. They are, when viewed in the first light, both the past and present invading this instant, the present. They are then the echoes of an ancestral heritage coming as they do from the great books of the Old Testament (cf. Is 64:1; 63:11; 42:1; Hos 11:11). They are also the future invading the now. They act as a summons. They have a teleological significance.

At the beginning Christ stands before darkness, chaos, the unformed. Entry to living is then entry into this darkness, this known and unknown, this paradox and mystery that is there before him. Nevertheless God has already spoken and this is what Mark is telling his readers. Who Christ is and his ultimate acceptance are already clearly stated by Mark. The self that he is stands at the center of the symbols that speak of him. He knows the meaning of these symbols in that they speak to him. Nevertheless it is only at the end of the Gospel, with the statement of the centurion, that we come to know fully who he really is.

Coming into the world, Jesus, as Mark presents him, remembers, and what he remembers is the Father, in his relationship to the other. He goes to John. He expects to hear condemnation and judgment. He is willing to enter in the dark. What he hears instead is acceptance, favor and the assurance of being the beloved one. The river Jordan provided what Rhoads calls a "threshold experience." It is a moment when his "transpersonal source is realized . . . a source which loves and supports him."[8]

What does all of this mean in terms of a story of the self? The poetic image of the baptism is mediating to me a reality of my existence. It is trying to pass on to me something about my life. It strives to give me knowledge that I should have but don't have. It speaks the essential. The symbols cluster together to speak to me: they are connecting me with the archetypes of my religious history. Wind, water, a voice, speak, and they speak the sacred. By entering them I enter the sacred. By listening to them I hear the sacred and I allow it to speak to me.

We pray now over this passage that wishes to speak through its symbols to us. I find myself as I enter into prayer going out to meet John the Baptist by the seashore. I am aware that I carry with me my own expectations. I carry them with me in bags and satchels. I bring with me to the seashore, each time I go, symbols of my way of living. I carry books to occupy my mind, blankets to mediate my comfort, food to satisfy my hunger and thirst, a radio so that I will not be alone, a hat for protection. I come to the water well insulated against anything really happening. Nevertheless I come hoping against hope, with some expectation that rest, relaxation, and water will help to change my life. I come in need of conversion, willing to be identified with the call to repentance.

John challenges my existence, my way of life. He stands on the sand, the barren sand, the hot sand. In fact, in my meditation he is the sand. He makes life uncomfortable, hosting the gnats and flies, the different bugs and insects that bite and chew and scratch at my comfort. He is the sand that gets into my hair and eyes and ears, that causes me to move from one side to the other, to slap at myself and tear at my extremities. He is the comforting sand that welcomes me out, then is too hot to lie on, too bumpy to rest on, too dazzling to look upon. He is the sand that knows the flotsam fragments of my life, the drifting strands of kelp, the broken twisted weeds, the gnarled wood. The sand is message, the sand is call, the sand is invitation.

"I must go down to the seas again, to the lonely sea and the sky," said the poet John Masefield, and so I arise to go from the sand to the water. As I enter into the water in my imagination I feel its coolness first, its distinctive difference from the sand. I feel it surround me and take on my shape. I have behind me all the symbols of my expectation clumped together on the beach. We cannot take our pasts into the water; it will not support them. At first I walk into the water carefully keeping my balance, carefully looking ahead for pitfalls. I realize how my past is not all on the beach. Some of it is still with me in my fears, cares, history. How can I get beyond the history? Is the water beloved lover, or cruel judge, the merciful upholder or the destroying power? Will she nourish or swallow? Somehow I know that I am called to enter her irrespective and let go.

In the water a shuddering, a shivering, a feeling, as my feet leave the safe ground, sweeps over me. It is an instant and a lifetime. It is like the shattering of the world, the rending of the sky in me. For one moment this ripping apart of me that anxiety is sweeps in upon me and holds me. And then a moment like no other. Somewhere beyond my fear, beyond my control, beyond both my desire and terror, I know I am afloat. Something in me is held by something even greater. The self that I am is addressed by the other that I am not and a voice that makes no sound speaks: "You are my beloved son: on you my favor rests."

Chapter 3
The Desert

There is something extraordinary about the Markan desert story that is immediately challenging, captivating and frightening. Reading it quickly one can pass over it without noticing how central it is to the Gospel. On the other hand, reading it slowly, one is left with very little to deal with. The advantage of reading it slowly is that it evokes all the other images of the desert that we have encountered. Nevertheless Mark's desert is unlike any of them. It is unlike the desert Moses entered. It has no burning bush to reveal the presence of God. Nobody speaks the divine name "Yahweh." It is unlike the desert Israel entered. There is no "fire by night or cloud by day." There is no water from the rock and no manna to eat. It is also unlike the desert of Isaiah which is going to bloom, and in which there will be placed "water" and "a way" for the chosen people. It's not like the desert of Hosea where God speaks to the heart and gives to his beloved the Valley of Achor as a door of hope. It is unlike the desert in which Israel becomes again the espoused. It's not even like the desert of Matthew and Luke where Jesus goes to be tempted

18

and encounters there the very possibility of turning aside from his mission. Mark's desert evokes all of these and yet it is unlike any of them.

Mark gives the following account of what happened to Jesus after the baptism. "At that point the Spirit sent him out toward the desert. He stayed in the wasteland forty days, put to the test there by Satan. He was with wild beasts, and angels waited on him" (1:12–13). The mention of forty days evokes the wandering of Israel in the desert. The fact that he was put to the test recalls the desert of the exile and Isaiah's story of its transformation as the exiles return. Jesus' being with wild beasts evokes the temptations of Matthew and Luke. When we are told that the angels waited on him we are given the impression of the desert of Hosea. Mark's desert touches all of them and yet it isn't any of them.

There is a radical simplicity about the Markan desert. He leaves out many details. There are no fires, clouds, rocks, water, no great stories or distractions, no powerful promises or temptations. He doesn't even occupy you with details of what Jesus wore or ate or anything like that. He omits even the details that the others suggest about the fasting. The details though brief, says Nineham, are meant to suggest that "Jesus was victorious but that this stage of the battle, though decisive, was not the final one; the struggle would continue in the various activities of Jesus during the ministry."[1] This is indeed true, and we get a definite struggle in the ministry of Jesus as the Gospel progresses. This absence of detail however has the interesting effect of placing the reader in the desert himself. It produces a desert-like atmosphere and the reader is brought face to face with it.

This desert has a surprising quality about it. Jesus is led there in spite of himself. In fact the text says that he is "driven." This is somewhat surprising. Secondly the text indicates, even though it does not spell it out, that the experience is one of ambivalence. He was "tempted by Satan," he was "with the beasts," and yet "angels ministered to him." There are two sides then to this desert. It is a story of challenge and endurance and a story of gift and support. Satan, beasts and angels are all symbols of realities that are encountered throughout Scripture. The first two are symbols of destruction, the third a symbol of divine sustenance and presence. The Markan desert has two sides to it.

Three further points can be made about the Markan desert. It is simple, it is silent, and it is filled with nothing. Reading the story leaves me with these impressions. This is the nature of the desert as it is encountered. Travelers who go to the desert frequently speak of these kinds of experiences. Jesus enters or is driven to that kind of experience. The result of it is that he next appears in "Galilee proclaiming the good news of God." This desert is a very unsatisfying experience from a reader's point of view. You want to do something with it, you want to shape it or fashion it or alter it. It nearly calls out to you to fulfill it, to fix it up, to change it in some way so you can work on it. The desert works on you wanting to work on it. It returns your face to you. It stares back, reminding one of the line in the close of Shelley's poem: ". . . boundless and bare/ The lone and level sands stretch far away."[2]

What does this mean in terms of a story of the self, or rather, put another way, what or when is the self confronted with this experience, namely of nothing? Perhaps there is a way of approaching and clarifying this event. Alan Jones makes a distinction between what he calls a desert and a wasteland. The two are different. In the wasteland, as he puts it, "much of the trouble we pass through is of our own making. The monsters we encounter have been

put together by our follies and machinations. The wasteland is largely our invention. There is however an intran-
sigence, a stubbornness about things which is given to us.
We do not conjure up all the troubles and monsters which
lie in our path. This recalcitrant and menacing givenness is
symbolized by the desert. The wasteland and the desert are
not identical. We make the wasteland for ourselves. The
desert is given to us. These two images point to the fact that
our condition is both given and manufactured."[3] Jones
points then to two kinds of situations, one where we man-
ufacture the problems, the other, the desert experience,
where we encounter the otherness of things.

The desert becomes the place of differentiation, and
because of that it is also the place of identity. This fits in
well with the desert experiences we have listed. It was in
the desert that Moses came to know the divine name; there
Israel discovered her identity, there she rediscovered herself in the years following the exile. That was Hosea's message. He was saying: the only way in which God can help
the people to realize who they are again is to take them into
the desert.

This is also true of the Markan desert. Jesus emerges
from it with a definite message, with a course and direction
for his life. It is for him a critical experience. The desert
however is not a single, once and for all, experience. It's not
that in the life of Israel, and it's not that in the life of Jesus
or his disciples. In the desert the messianic secret returns.
Who Christ is remains hidden in something or someone
more ultimate than himself. There he chooses to be supported by that transcendence beyond himself. There he
appears, as later events more clearly show, to choose a
relatedness to all the events that life brings him.

Thus far I have used a series of words that seem to me
to describe the desert experience from a Markan point of

view. They are: simple, surprising, silent, empty, ambivalent, a place of differentiation, and a sense of otherness—
all leading to a consequent sense of mission. Is that like
anything in life? Jung points to a divided state when com-
peting impulses catch the ego. It is here, he says, that the
horizons of man's life are expanded, that conflict begins to
erupt, that life is hassled with inferiority feelings, sexual
impulses, etc. Here a man begins to grapple with his own
identity and forge his own personality. Who am I? These
are the questions that emerge. Evelyn Whitehead and James
Whitehead comment, "Who am I? Who am I with? What
should I do? What does it all mean? These questions can be
asked at several levels. . . . These are the perennial questions of human experience never fully resolved or finally
answered. . . . During adolescence who am I is paramount. . . . During mature years of late adulthood, what
does it all mean? . . . During the long period of early and
middle adulthood, who am I with and how am I with people? . . . In the mid years, what can I do, what should I do?"[4]
These years then are years of struggle. They come not once
but many times to life. They are moments not of our own
making but they can be aggravated by our own making.
Basically however they are moments into which we are led
by life itself. In these moments or spaces we face limits, ultimacy, and meaning.

I am drawn and driven to the desert. There I must go,
even though I may not want to go, because there is no other
way. This is the way of life. I enter it and immediately touch
its ambivalence, its warm burning days, its cold empty
nights, and in both, although in different ways, I become
aware of my own loneliness, my own questions. Here I
touch the frustration of many appetites, the heated passions
that burn unabated and mingle with the coldness of a life
emptied of passion. I discover that I have brought all of me

to this empty wasteland and there met all of it, and it is desert, and it is deserted. Its emptiness infuriates my loneliness, and my turmoil cries out to its presence, and I question if it is faceless, empty and impersonal. Here I touch upon the reality that I am alone even if I am with others, and that while our edges touch and mingle we are not the same. They are different. They are not me. They are other. Nevertheless they are connected in some strange way also; they are part of the single fabric that life is.

Standing still in silence is disquieting and unnerving. Everything invades the vacuum created by the stillness. The restless patterns of desire rise to the surface. Old bones, messages of former histories and ages, are discovered in the desert sands. Subjectivity and objectivity mix, detach and return. I am already part of a story that is unfolding without me. I am part of a universe that seems to have a destiny and purpose apart from me, and so I wonder if my existence affects that in any way. I am myself already unfolding in response to the surrounding story, and so I wonder if I am free. I am within a story of time and space, of ambition, prejudice, and failure, and I wonder where my "innocence" will take me. Here in the youthful years of the desert the edges of stories meet and I wonder about story, my story and how it will be, and what I want it to be, and how I can make it be. Michael Novak puts it well when he says, "The question 'what ought we to desire' comes down to what identity we wish to give ourselves. Who are we? We make ourselves who we are; we invent ourselves. What is it then we desire to desire? What is the model we are imitating? What goals have we set for ourselves? . . . I am not my body. I am not my passions. I am not my mind. I am I. What we need today, most earnestly, is a way of imagining intelligence that is not objectifying, manipulative, alienating; a way of feeling within oneself the coursing of one's blood, the aliveness of one's nerves, the power of one's passions, the labyrinthine intricacies of one's perceptions . . . and still of acting intelligently. We need models of passionate intelligence, intelligent passion."[5]

The desert experience comes many times in a life. We return to it again and again. Frequently Jesus will go to the desert to be alone, to pray. On occasion he will take others there. In Mark this experience nearly always precedes a new turning point in his life. He emerges from the desert with a new purpose or a renewed vision: he emerges with a new-found energy. It reminds me of the poem of Merrit Molloy entitled "Mohawk Ridge":

> I used to think I went there
> Because I wanted to be alone
> Later I found I went there because
> I was alone.[6]

The desert confuses, twists, forces questions together. It upsets our normal vision and forces us to see things in different arrangements. In the desert the self reaches out into the nothingness and even through the nothingness to touch its goal, its transcendent source. To do this however it must let go of all that holds it down, that holds it fettered. We must let go of mother and father, not just biological mothers and fathers but the mother and father figures. As Alan Jones puts it, "Wombless and motherless we are stuck with the fearsome givenness of things, the isness of life. The isness often oppresses us. We feel hemmed in by the limitations of time and space. We feel there is no freedom, only fate."[7]

The desert in Mark is a short scene. Nevertheless it is a profoundly important scene. Its simplicity, its lack of development by Mark, etc., as we have noted, gives us a

feeling of being in the desert. His insistence on its importance gives me a sense of how crucial it is. His drawing
Jesus to it frequently imparts a sense of its repetitiveness in
my life. Finally the lack of any development leaves it as a
question for me. This perhaps, however, is also a clue; the
desert is the question in my life.

Chapter 4
The Call

Mark now turns his attention to unfolding for us the life of Jesus, and the first incident he selects is the call of the fishermen. These are to be his disciples. It is important to note right away that there is something different about this call. The disciples are not like other disciples. There is a difference. Normally the student or disciple goes in search of the master. They go and seek someone who will teach them the way to truth, or the way to wisdom, etc. Here the order is reversed. It is Jesus who calls them. For Mark discipleship starts with Jesus. He looks, he approaches, he summons, he calls. All the verbs indicate his initiation. They follow.

Those whom he calls seem to have no special training. They are fishermen. At first only four are called. They belong to two different families. Then others are called, until eventually there are twelve and this band becomes known as the "disciples." There is, it appears, a core group within this band, and in Mark they are the only ones that speak throughout the Gospel. They are Simon Peter, James and John. Even within this group it is obvious that there is a key figure. "Even if Mark had not told us that Peter was called to discipleship first and had not named Peter first in the list of the twelve, these passages would make it clear that, for Mark, Peter was the most prominent among the twelve in the Gospel picture of Jesus' ministry. In 1:35–38, 8:27–33, 10:28–30, 11:12–22, 14:27–31, and 16:7, while other disciples or members of the twelve are mentioned, or are on the scene, special attention is focused on Peter."[1] These apostles or disciples play a prominent part in this story. Their function will be clarified as the story unfolds and each scene will add to the overall picture. Initially they are cast in a favorable light but as the story develops they appear to undergo a change.[2] There are, it appears, two sides to their discipleship. They exhibit loyalty in leaving everything to follow him: they accept the ministry of healing and exorcising in his name. They carefully attend to his teaching and try to grasp what it is he is telling them. They are by his side in Galilee, in Jerusalem, and at the Last Supper. All of this, and more, constitutes the positive and indeed preferential side of their existence. The disciples then are in a privileged position. They are intimates of Jesus, sharing in his life and mission. They carry forward his message. They are his agents. They are his confidants and his closest and most intimate friends.[3]

But there is another side to this life they have with Jesus. Their life reflects a dark side, a shadow side as Theodore Weeden has carefully pointed out.[4] They are constantly cast in the light of not understanding. They get in the way. They don't grasp the meaning of the feedings in the desert, the stilling of the storms, the predictions of the passion. They seem to be constantly cast in a role of fear, anxiety and apprehension. They are worried about themselves, their power, position and status, and in the end Jesus will have to accuse them of being blind and deaf. We will see more of this in later chapters, but it is important to draw it into our awareness from the beginning since it is part of the discipleship picture.

In terms of a story of the self we must now learn what discipleship could mean. What is it that is both an ally of the self but that also casts a shadow, what is it that helps the self in its mission but also seems to have a dark side? We see Jesus in this chapter calling to his aid four assistants who will do the following: learn from him, become his disciples, be with him, carry forth his message, act in his name, manifest his goodness, and become an offer of salvation to all people. The summons of Christ is a call to be his disciples. At the same time it is a call to become his apostles. One must first follow before one can lead. What is it that is called to listen to the self before it is called to act in the name of the self? Is there anything in me that corresponds to the disciples that are summoned by the Christ to follow him?

Jung says that the self is the center and goal of the individuation process. The self initiates the process of individuation, of movement toward wholeness in the personality, and at the same time it is the goal of the process. In the first half of this process the self must incarnate. To do this it must free itself from the sea, from what Eric Neumann calls the uroboric state. As the ego begins to form out of the unconscious there is initially "no continuous memory; at most there are islands of consciousness which are like single lamps or lighted objects in the far flung darkness."[5] Isn't this what is happening in the story? Peter, Andrew, James and John see Jesus, hear Jesus and take off and the whole thing makes no sense. They leave the sea and all that it stands for, and indeed the sea is often in mythology a symbol of the unconscious. Jesus makes his way along the sea and calls them forth. The whole lack of sense in the story can be grasped if you put yourself in Zebedee's position. He sees his sons walk away. They have no connection (memory) of Jesus, they have no ties to him (therefore it's chaotic, it doesn't fit that they would up and leave), yet they are drawn to him, to follow him and to be his disciples. Something breaks out of the sea of the unconscious to which it is moored and establishes itself in relation to the self even though as yet there is only a very germinal ego-self axis, disciple-master axis.

Not only are they called but the Scriptures say that there are four of them and that they are now given titles or designations. Jesus will make them "fishers of men." Jung says that in life we need to develop masks which help us to adapt to our society. This he calls the persona. The persona helps me in my project of living, but if I become totally identified with the persona then there will be problems. The persona is important in the early stages of life. In fact the task is to establish one, but the persona is itself the result of something. It comes about as I develop a way of relating to the world, of taking in the world, of evaluating the world and of responding to the world—which in fact is exactly what Jesus appears to be teaching the disciples. Jung believed that all people are biologically predisposed, that is, that from birth they have a certain attitudinal preference for dealing with life.[6] Thus from the beginning some are extroverts who turn out to the world with open arms. Others are introverts who will be predisposed from birth to enter into the inner world of their own thoughts, feelings, etc. For the introvert the subjective elements will be determinative.

As I look to the story of the call of the disciples in Mark I find that the story helps me to discover something about me. Who is the "I" that is called by the self? Who are the disciples in me? What do they correspond to, or how are they now alive in me? My eyes fasten on the extroverted stance of the apostles. The four who are mentioned in this story are the four who throughout the Gospel speak, heal, and exorcise in his name. They are the ones who relate to the world in the Gospel. They are the ones who feed the multitude, and who communicate with the crowds. They are the only ones who speak. The other disciples, though present, are not presented by Mark as speaking. Theirs is a hidden and quieter kind of presence. The flow of energy from the four presented in the story is outward. They are the first to speak in response to many events—e.g., when Jesus talks of the cross in 8:31, Peter immediately rebukes him; when Jesus is transfigured before them, Peter imme-diately wants to stay (9:5); when Jesus asks who people say he is, Peter jumps in quickly with an answer (8:29), etc. They are the ones who want to get things done. They want to know why they can't relate to some and they can to oth-ers (9:14). They don't like surprises, especially painful ones, as is evidenced by their response to the passion predictions (cf. 8:31; 9:31; 10:31). They seem more at home around people and fall asleep when they are alone with Jesus, e.g., Gethsemani. To me they present an extroverted stance. They call forth that in me. They speak to that side of me. The other disciples speak more to the introverted me, but more of that later.

Secondly as I look at them in this story and throughout the Gospel they seem to me to be intuitive. They are very quick in this story to grasp onto something about Jesus. They see something that Zebedee apparently doesn't see, and whatever that is, it makes a great impression on them. Jesus is passing along the sea and calls to them, and they follow him immediately, and that's strange and wonderful. People don't do that easily. They question strangers and try to find out where they came from, what they want, what they will get out of it, why they should go, etc. There is none of that here. To get the feeling of how strange and unusual it is you need to pray the story from Zebedee's point of view because then the whole ludicrous nature of the thing becomes apparent. Tom Kane remarks, "We are dealing here with the unspeakable, literally unimaginable, hope that comes upon us from beyond and that is the fruit of God's healing and creative love. For that reason theologians would name it an eschatological call. . . . [The apostles] can't tell you what has happened. But what their hearts have always longed for, what they have looked for in the wrong place opens up before them in a flash. They follow him."[7] The familiar and present scents, tastes, smells of the sea can't hold them. The nets, fish, and even the family ties are not as important. The past must be thrown away, the family left behind, the familiar discarded. There is a recklessness here as the new, with its possibilities, comes crashing into their lives. This is further evidenced in the rest of the Gospel when they launch themselves, without thinking, into new and different situations—e.g., the feeding stories, the storm on the lake, the transfiguration, etc. They follow their hunch, which is their glory, but had they been more sensitive as well, things may have been different. In fact we will see the more conservative element emerge in the conflict stories.

On a third level they come across to me as men of feeling. They obviously were very aware of their feelings in such stories as the storm on the lake (4:35–41), the walking on the water (6:45–52), the predictions of the cross (8:31), etc. They are perplexed when he tells them to feed the people, amazed when he teaches them, frightened when he leaves them, and delighted when he is with them. They are in a joyful mood when he eats with them as at the Last Supper, and discouraged when he suffers, and finally they are brokenhearted when he dies. When Jesus tries to teach them, or draws them into a discussion to explain to them things about the Kingdom, they are mesmerized and so frequently miss the point of his teaching that he accuses them of being deaf and blind and having their hearts hardened. They seem to like things going nicely, when there is a sense of harmony and togetherness, and there is a sense of joy in them when everyone is looking for Jesus after the healing in Peter's mother-in-law's house. At the same time they jealously guard their own uniqueness and group. They don't want anyone else "not of their company" doing miracles (9:37). They become indignant with James and John when it is discovered that they want the best seats (10:41). They enjoy the good times with Jesus, but their feelings of fear and anxiety lead them to abandon him during the passion. All of the words associated with Jung's thinking type seem difficult for them—e.g., principle, objective, analysis, justice, impersonal, etc. While all the words associated with the feeling type seem to me to reflect their stance in the Gospel—e.g., sympathy, devotion, humane, personal, harmony, subjective, intimacy, persuasion, etc.

On a fourth and final level, looking at the call, we begin to glimpse another factor about the apostles. They seem to have a fairly flexible life style. In some ways they are surely people who like closure. Peter does want to tie things down at the transfiguration, and he does want to know and be guaranteed his reward in 10:28; but my sense of their presence in an overall way is more of adaptability and flexibility. They do leave Zebedee and the nets and adapt to a new way of life. They do accept what Jesus says even if they don't understand. They do await further clarification regarding the cross and the Kingdom. They don't seem to need to have all the answers. They are indeed curious, and probe and question, but they await the further revelation. They seem to have difficulty with decisions because of that; they don't know what to do if he isn't around and so panic in the storm, go to sleep in the garden, and desert him at the crucifixion. They are on the other hand willing to adapt, to let go of Zebedee and the nets to follow him, then to leave Capernaum and go with him, then to follow him around the lake, then to settle for life at the transfiguration, etc. They miss things that perhaps need to be accomplished, either because no one told them, or it just never occurred to them—e.g., to bring bread for everybody. They don't seem to be interested in connecting their experiences together in logical order, content more to follow their hunch, and then adapt to what develops.

The Gospel story helps me to discover something about myself in my reading of this call of the disciples and my identification with them. Others may read their presence differently, and indeed the ongoing debate about the disciples in Mark merely testifies to that fact.[8] I see the disciples in the way described above. My eyes are attuned to those aspects in the Gospel quickly and without great effort. They say as much about me and my preferences as they do about the disciples. Here eisogesis and exegesis mix together in meditation, in prayer, in creative imagination, or rather in what Jung calls "active imagination." Only here the active imagination is upon the apostles as received sumbols in me. The establishment of these aspects of our personality, as we shall see, is important, because, as Christopher Grannis puts it, "the journey of faith begins at the Lord's invitation: he finds us in our places of marginal existence—in our personal Galilees—where we hunger for good news and the promise of liberation. . . . Our lives, our ways of seeing, judging, and acting are transformed by Christ as we experience his reign in our midst. We need to give ourselves over to the process of conversion and to be taught the path of discipleship."[9]

Chapter 5
A Typical Day

Mark now turns to what Scripture scholars call a "typical day in the life of Jesus."[1] In this day we are going to perceive what Jesus was normally doing during his lifetime. This is the work that is characteristic of him. It is a kind of microcosm of the macrocosm, a segment that illustrates the whole. In it we will see in a general way what Jesus will be about in his life. The stories of this day indicate that (1) he is a teacher who brings a new vision to those he meets, who speaks with authority and whose teaching is authoritative in a new way; (2) he is a healer who brings to the sick his own presence in such a way that it frees them for service to the community as a whole: (3) he is one who is connected to a greater mystery; (4) he relates to the larger community but does not allow that larger community either to dictate or to define his life. His then is a movement of freedom toward freedom; he moves to share with others the good news of his own freedom. He does this by freeing the energies that are locked up in demons, scapegoats, outcasts and the like. He brought these energies into a relationship with

him, and in discovering this they were freed to do what
they willed to do.

Immediately in the very first of the stories Mark turns
to the authority of Jesus. He does not indicate, stress, or
dwell upon the content of his teaching. It is the authority of
the person himself that catches his attention. Nineham indicates that the teaching of the scribes was almost wholly
derivative and consisted in repeating the opinions of their
predecessors.[2] Jesus' teaching is never merely this kind of
teaching. It is this at times but is always more than this.
Bornkam points out that Jesus' teaching does correspond
with that of a rabbi in the way he discusses with his opponents. Yet he doesn't "study" in the school of a famous
rabbi; indeed his adversaries call him unlearned. He doesn't
claim for himself the authority of the fathers. He moves
about with an informality which does not fit the picture and
custom of a rabbi, and he does enter into open conflict with
the law.[3] There is about Jesus, however, something very
special which can only be characterized by saying that he
spoke with authority. This is noticeable and perceivable. In
fact in the Gospel it is not only people who notice this but
also nature, demons, sickness, etc. Sickness surrenders to it
(1:29), the storm quiets down at his command (4:35), the
demons leave when instructed (1:26), the dead even
respond when summoned (5:35). His authority then is per-
vasive. Its effect on people is most noticeable. Those who
are his opponents plot and plan against him precisely
because of it. The apostles on the other hand are just awe-
struck and amazed by it constantly, while others in the Gospel are both astonished and frightened by it (5:33).

Nevertheless there is also a limit to Jesus' authority.
While this is not clearly indicated in this typical day, it is
hinted at in that he must go to be alone and in prayer. It is

spelled out, however, in the rest of the Gospel. There are things that he cannot do as when he tells the sons of Zebedee that he cannot assure them places at his side in the Kingdom, or like the time he indicates his limited knowledge in 13:32. He does not know "the exact day or hour" when "these things will come to pass." "Neither the angels in heaven nor the Son, but only the Father knows" that time.

We can also notice that there is a rhythm and pattern to the day which is followed through the Gospel. This can briefly be described as follows: Jesus moves between being in public and being in private, between being with and present to his disciples and absent and away from them, from being a healer of others to one who must be supported and healed himself (in his presence to the Father), from being with men to being with and including women, from being in battle with the forces and energy of evil to being with friends in celebration. It is in the movement of this day and in these patterns that we see Jesus dealing with and revealing and exposing attitudes relative to life and death, pain, celebration, suffering, joy, intimacy, mastery, discovery, loss, etc. We see here the dynamics of choosing and renouncing, confronting and affirming, attachment and detachment, etc. There is in this day a movement between what we might call God in Jesus' story, and Jesus in God's story, and the movement asks us to become aware of the pattern of our own lives.

Turning then to the first story, we see that it is a tale of exorcism. There are four such stories in the Gospel, three of them coming in the first half (1:23, 5:1, 7:24, and 9:14). Right away we can notice that this story is a battle, and the battle is for structure. The unclean spirit is trying to gain control over Jesus, to eliminate and subdue him, to be himself the controlling power. Scripture scholars reflect this battle by pointing to the chiastic structure of the passage. This type of structure emphasizes the center part and distributes parallel ideas in the outer parts. Thus the passage would read as follows:

> Demons: What have you to do with us Jesus of Nazareth. Have you come to destroy us?
>
> Jesus: Come out of him.
>
> Demons: I know who you are. The Holy One of God.
>
> Jesus: Be silent.

The initiative in all four exorcisms in the Gospel is taken by someone other than Jesus. His presence is itself the invitation. Here the initiative is taken by the evil spirit who attempts to name Christ. This is an event of considerable importance since to name something, in biblical terms, is to own it, to control it, to have it as one's possession. It is an attempt to absorb it. It is indeed a kind of magical way of taking its power under one's control. Schnackenberg points out how in ancient history "the exorcist makes a counterattack and tries with adjuration formulas and magic means to master the demon to force him to leave the possessed man."[4] Against the background of such an approach the originality and uniqueness of Jesus' actions in the spectator's eyes of that time become apparent. Jesus does without magic words and magic means, and commands the unclean spirit with a mere word of command. It is Christ then who wins the battle for structure; it is his command, his authority that is the greater. Lightfoot comments that Mark places the story here in this prominent position because he "wishes to emphasize that one great purpose of the coming

of the Messiah was the extinction of the powers of evil."[5]
Jesus is an offer of salvation, and an authoritative one at
that.

    Seen as a story of the self, this section of the Gospel
helps us to understand what growth will be about in life. It
means there must be a meeting between the self and the
other aspects of the personality. There will be a dynamic
movement, an interplay between these during one's life
story. I try to incarnate my self in the world. Initially this
incarnation of myself is in opposition to some forces of the
world, the powers of evil. This antagonism is an apparent
antagonism between them and me. However as I look at
them I begin to see that the demons of the outer world are
really carriers of the demons of the inner world. The very
endeavor to incarnate myself in the world confronts me
with the question of who I am and who I am not. It forces
me to open to the mystery of who I am. I will be brought
to a confrontation between the demon that seeks to control
my life and the self that is the truly authoritative voice. Hillman puts it as follows: "The cure of the shadow is, on the
one hand, a moral problem; that is, recognition of what we
have repressed, how we perform our repressions, how we
rationalize and deceive ourselves, what sort of goals
we have, and what we have hurt, even maimed, in the
name of these goals. On the other hand the cure of the
shadow is a problem of love. How far can our goal extend
to the broken and ruined parts of ourselves, the disgusting
and perverse? . . . If we approach ourselves to cure these
fixed intractable congenital weaknesses of stubborness and
blindness, of meanness and cruelty, of shame and pomp,
we come up against a new way of being together in which
ego must serve and listen and cooperate with a host of
shadowy unpleasant figures and discover an ability to love
even the least of these traits."[6]

The story that we read is a story that takes place in the public domain. Frequently too this is where I will first encounter the demons of my life. They will be the other, the inferior, the scapegoat, the minority, the communist, the different, the other than I. Generally the key to the scapegoat, to the projection, is the affect. In this story the demon "shrieks." The affect is a clue. In fact the demon recognizes the Christ as the Christ recognizes the demon. The battle between the two is engaged and the issue is clearly who is in charge. Life then will grow and develop as I enter the battle and catch the shadows and demons. I must (1) perceive the demon, (2) claim the demon (3) name the demon, (4) tame the demon, (5) reaim the energies locked up in the demon. This is part of the typical day's work if one is to grow and see in his own story the story of Jesus.

In the second story of this day's work Mark shifts the emphasis. He goes from the public level of the first story to the private level of the second, and he also goes from a story of a man to one involving a woman. He goes from a story involving words to one involving action only, from a story that happens in the synagogue to one that happens on the way out. In Mark Jesus meets a number of women. Significantly enough most of them are presented as wounded in some way. Peter's mother-in-law is sick with fever (1:30), the Syro-phoenician woman is worried about her daughter who has an evil spirit (7:26), the woman who touches his garment has a twelve-year hemorrhage (5:29), the official's daughter is apparently dead (5:34), Herodias and her daughter are presented as somewhat less than well adjusted people who plot and plan together against their husband and father respectively (6:21). On the other hand in the second half of the Gospel the women appear to fare considerably better, the widow is praised for her contribution (12:41), the woman of Bethany anoints him for burial

(14:3), the women at the tomb come to anoint him (16:1). In the second half then, even though still wounded, they are more specifically mentioned as coming to his aid. Within this particular story of Chapter 1 it is noteworthy to see how these qualities are already present. Peter's mother-in-law is first of all sick with fever, a drain and worry on the apostles since it's the first thing that occurs to them to tell him. Then he heals her and she finally ends up with an act of service which Schweizer is quick to point out is the specific manner of discipleship for a woman.[7] It is then the story of a wounded woman who exists on the fringes of the apostolic group, related to them (she is Peter's mother-in-law), and now being brought into contact with Jesus.

We all have an old woman within. In fact we all have many women within us who live at the fringe level of our life. They have not yet been brought into the service of the personality where their energies can serve and nourish, strengthen and develop the personality. Jung called these figures the anima (women have within them figures of the masculine which he calls the animus). Whitmont sees the anima as a kind of married partner in each of us that must be given attention and consideration, discipline and challenge. For the growth of the personality to fullness he says, it is "necessary to find out what this other personality is like, how it feels, thinks and tends to act."[8] She must then be brought into consciousness. While she is resident in the unconscious she is in control of the personality. When she is admitted into the "household of consciousness then she becomes the eros of consciousness . . . [giving] relationship and relatedness to [his] consciousness. In this negotiation man is no longer possessed by his anima; rather he learns to receive her, to grant her a certain space in his being, especially in giving shape to his relationships."[9] Man then in becoming conscious of this anima figure is enriched and a change of attitude toward the feminine is frequently evidenced.

Marie Von Franz indicates that there are four faces to the anima, and we can describe these briefly as follows. The first face is the face "of Eve which represents purely unstructured and biological relations. The second personifies a romantic and aesthetic level that is still characterized by sexual elements. The third is represented by the Virgin Mary . . . a figure who raises love to the heights of spiritual devotion. The fourth is symbolized by Sapientia, wisdom, transcending the most holy and most pure."[10] The anima will not be ignored. She will have her say. If we try to ignore her we do so to our own detriment. If we pay attention, then she can reveal new possibilities, new potentialities for service and incarnation. She provides, however, not only new possibilities for man, but, as Jung says, she "lures him into life's frightening paradoxes and ambivalences where good and evil, success and ruin, hope and despair counterbalance one another."

Praying, meditating, reflecting then on these women in Mark can perhaps begin to put me in touch with some of this. To come in contact with the anima is part of the work of growth, of life. It is part of what we are attempting to see in and through the Jesus story. I look upon this woman in the house as I enter it in my prayerful imagination with Peter and Jesus. I notice the woman as she is pointed out to me. What is she like as she lies sick in the bed? Is she passive? Active? Does she move toward me or away from me? Is she engaging or disengaging? Does she reach out physically, emotionally, or spiritually? Is she silent or withdrawn? Is she anxious, frightened or fearful? Is she hopeful or accepting? What feelings does she trigger in me as I look upon her in the bed?

As a story of the self, the mother-in-law is an image of a dimension in me, a mood, emotion, etc., that is either positive or negative. Something about this mood or emotion is wounded, is feverish, is hurting; something about it is drawing from rather than adding to my possibilities for life. It's crying out to be integrated. I think of Teilhard de Chardin and how the feminine dimension gave to his thought a depth and richness. His search for an exclusive God of iron gave way to a deeper reality with his awakening to the feminine. He tells us himself that he was awakened to the immensity of life, to a way of seeing a sort of "shimmer of precious fabric . . . beneath the accidental determinations of existence."[11] I think of Dante awakening to find himself in a "dark wood where the right road was wholly lost and gone," going through the desert and encountering the leopard, the lion and the lamb, and the coming to know Beatrice through whom he comes to know the love that moves the sun and all the other stars."[12] Through their discovery of the feminine they were freed. In this typical day I begin to see that the way forward for me will also involve this meeting with the feminine, this encounter with the anima within.

In the third vignette Mark returns to the desert that we mentioned earlier. Most Scripture scholars pass relatively quickly over this little episode. Schweizer comments briefly that verse 35 underscores the fact that prayer was an essential part of his service and that it guarded that service from overactivity as well as indolence. It was at the same time a refuge from an enthusiastic recognition on the part of individuals who did not desire to become disciples.[13] The story tells of the absence of Jesus. He is gone from the disciples, or at least they don't know where he is and they must go in search of him. It is clear that they are not the only ones who miss him. "Everybody is looking for you" is their remark upon finding him. It also appears that while from

their point of view his absence appears catastrophic, from
his point of view it is essential. To fully understand this we
would need to see it as a single piece with his other times
of prayer in Mark.

There are two other mentions of Jesus' prayer in Mark;
after the multiplication of the loaves (6:46) and in Gethsemani (14:35). Harrington points out that on each occasion
the "nature of Jesus' messiahship is in question and he has
to contend with the incomprehension of his disciples."[14]
Prayer is where Jesus reveals the intensity of his relationship to the Father; it's where we glimpse who he is in his
own inner reality. His authority, his healings, his actions,
all flow from this relationship.

Does the absence of Jesus speak of anything in my life?
The observation of Viktor Frankl provides a possible clue.
He says, "Starting from man's meaning orientation, i.e., his
will to meaning, we have arrived at another problem,
namely his meaning confrontation. The first issue refers to
what man basically is: oriented toward meaning; the second
refers to what he should be: confronted with meaning."[15]
Throughout the history of mankind there are moments
where meaning seems to have left, where there seems to be
no purpose at all to history. Individuals too go through
these times when, as Yeats put it, "Things fall apart; the
center cannot hold."[16] Such are moments in which we face
the black hole of existence, the apparent loss of self. Frequently this experience follows or precedes some momentous life decision. It is as if there is a shift in the gestalt, and
instead of the self being the background that lights up the
foreground, something else becomes the background. A
desperate and frequently a despondent kind of nihilism
takes over. The person I am, the life I live, the values I witness to become gray, clouded, shrouded in a darkness I
don't fully understand. Over me then comes a feeling of

nothingness, a void, a barrenness. I can sense the absence of the self, and need to go in search again. Nouwen speaks of three conversions or rather of one conversion in a three-fold process, as a change from "suffocating loneliness to receptive solitude, from hostility to hospitality, and from illusion to prayer."[17] This is the kind of change that occurs, that begins to occur, in the lifetime and growth of one who senses the absence of self and pays attention to it.

In the story Jesus decides to move on. His return signals a fresh start. He points to a new and larger horizon. He breaks through to a larger world, and as he does they are again captivated and follow him. In fact each time Jesus goes to the desert and enters into prayer it is a moment of tension, each time it is an experience of existential loneliness, and each time it is followed by an enlarged horizon. Kelber comments that "Simon and the other disciples notice his absence in Capernaum and they are reported to have 'pursued him.' The point is not that Simon and the others follow Jesus as loyal disciples, but rather they seek after him. . . . What they have in mind is Jesus' return to Capernaum, the site of his earliest triumphs. Everyone is looking for you. What Jesus has in mind however is to move elsewhere. . . . The disciples wish to repeat the glory of the feast day while Jesus is oriented toward new places and the future."[18]

The first story we meet, at the end of the typical day, is about a leper. It's an interesting story in that the leper is an outcast of society. The law ostracized him and forced him to live apart from the community. Furthermore it laid upon him the rather undignified responsibility of proclaiming himself unclean to all the world so that they could avoid being contaminated by him (cf. Lev 13:45). Harrington reminds us that in "the New Testament the removal of leprosy is never described as healing but always as cleansing."[19] This fact helps us understand that uncleanness and dirtiness is associated with the leper. He is regarded as a source of defilement not only for himself but also for others who contact him. This disease then involves, like no other, exclusion from the community. There is a great depth of emotion involved in the story. The leper is portrayed as "coming," "beseeching," "kneeling" and saying to Jesus. All of these words point to his need, to his inferior position, to his situation. Jesus on the other hand is seen in positive terms as being moved with anger (many translate this as pity), stretching toward, "touching" and saying—then commanding sternly. Lightfoot offers an explanatory comment that Jesus is not angry with the individual leper but with the pitiful condition of helpless humanity.

In the story my eyes get drawn to the leper. I notice right away his amazing courage. He is a man who is not afraid to take risks. He is not afraid to approach Jesus even though there is a crowd around him. He is not afraid to be thought of as a fool by others: he is not that concerned about their thinking. I am immediately put in touch with my own security. I begin to recognize how differently I might respond. I catch just for a moment how really ostracized I am myself. I am ruled by other things, by fear of what others think, or say, or do. I allow those fears to prevent my deeper freedom. I allow them to interfere with my coming to the center where I believe I can be healed and freed. I stand at the edges alone.

Then my eyes move to Christ and I see his freeing presence; his life is an invitation. He doesn't do or say anything. He himself is welcome and hospitality. I recognize something deep down in me beyond my fears; something begins to stir and I find myself moving toward it. I am not sure who or what it is. It has no names, no titles, no public sign other than its existence. Nevertheless it is goodness. I sense that and I recognize my need to live there and to bring my fears there.

I find myself caught between this security that I think I have, that is really an illusion, and this other attraction that lies just beyond me. I know that to ask is the first step but I find it difficult. My eyes catch the leper as he kneels on his twisted stumps and reaches with his amputated arms. I notice how difficult it is to bring my fears to their knees, yet everything in me wants to be freed. I wonder if I will be taken seriously, not knowing how my fears are so obvious already. I wonder if I will be laughed at, not knowing how easily now I am pitied. I wonder if I will be given charity, in the negative sense, not fully realizing how so pitifully my own passivity makes anything else impossible.

I look at the leper and through him to the eyes of Jesus again. Is he tough and rough, is he demanding and uncompromising, is he bloodless and gutless? For one panicky moment I think he will never understand. And then I see his hands coming toward me, embracing me, accepting me, and speaking to me. He forbids my fears to speak again, and in truth the leper doesn't speak. I recognize a depth in me that acknowledges that I am frightened, and fearful, and isolated. I come home and it's worth the coming home.

Coming away from my meditation I find a new freedom in me and I take my pen in hand and write the good news of what I have discovered. It comes out as follows:

I am the I I am not
I am not the I I am
I am the life emerging
And I am the requiem
I am the I I am not
For I am the I I am.

Chapter 6
Conflict

Now that Mark has given his readers an overview of what the life of Jesus is going to involve he begins to flesh it out in more detail. He places Jesus immediately in the midst of conflict. This is a clever technique which permits Mark to accomplish a number of purposes. It helps him to advance the drama. It gets the reader's attention, and finally it catapults the reader into his own story.[1] As I watch the drama I am encouraged to leave the position of spectator looking at the event from outside. I feel called to begin asking within me the question that the drama exposes and then to see with the eyes of Mark as he moves Jesus through the five stories.

In these five stories of conflict the opponents in question are the scribes, Pharisees and Herodians. This contrasts with the opponents in the later conflict stories of Chapter 12. There the opponents will be representatives of the strictly religious viewpoint. Here the conflict is between Jesus and his disciples on the one hand and the scribes, etc., on the other. They will express the condemnatory judgment of the majority, or, putting it another way, they will express the expectation of the collective. The stories then clearly reflect a battle for authority, and the very arrangement of the material itself shows the growing energy of the opposition and the insistent statements of Jesus holding to his viewpoint. The structure reflects the action. First "the legal experts are introduced, then the legal experts of the Pharisees, then the Pharisees with the Herodians. First the opponents accuse Jesus in thought only, then they question the disciples about Jesus' action, then they question Jesus about an offense against a custom, after that they question Jesus about the illegal behavior of the disciples, then they watch Jesus in order to get charges against him, and finally they go off to plot and destroy him. As opposition propels the action forward Jesus' response intensifies."[2]

The structure of the five stories not only reflects an intensification of energy and a building of opposition but it also reflects a centering, a coring. The demands and expectations of the collective move toward the center and the structure reflects this movement. There are five stories and they are carefully arranged around the center story. This lends its energies to the other four stories so that there is a movement back and forth from the center to the periphery. The five stories are enlightened by, and in turn illuminate, the center story:

> Stories one and five are related in many ways. They both involve cures, both involve a part of the body that is healed, both stories take place indoors, and in both stories there is a delay. Finally in both we have the same cast of characters, Jesus, the authorities and the sick person.
>
> Stories two and four are likewise linked. Both stories have to do with eating and in both there is the under-

lying question of uncleanness. Here also you have the same cast of characters in both stories, Jesus, the disciples and authorities.

The third story by contrast stands alone. It radiates meaning however to the other four stories as spokes to a wheel. The centrality of Jesus stands out here. The conflict seems to have been resolved. The characters here ask a more open ended question and the response of Jesus is much more elaborate. At the center the conflict is resolved.

From yet a third vantage point the five stories in their structural arrangement have something to say to us. The first two stories have as a theme the question of forgiveness, with the receiving into a relationship with Jesus those who were considered outcasts who can authorize that kind of move. The fourth and fifth stories have to do with worship, with the sabbath, with praise, with holiness and honoring God. This leaves the third story again as central, and here it is the presence of the bridegroom, the newness of Jesus, the importance of the center that is highlighted. The five stories then in their structural arrangement, whether in terms of the direction of energy, or in terms of their "concentric patterning,"[3] or in terms of their linear progression, all point to the central importance of conflict. Whatever the story is about, it seems to hook the opponents into a conflict with Jesus about authority. In our growth in life each of us must do battle with our complexes until we have brought them into consciousness. As long as the impulses are unconscious and we are identical with them they own us and the drive or impulse is at its most harmful. These stories can help us perhaps to come in contact with our own authority complex. They help us to come in contact with the central authority of the self and to discover areas of opposition within the personality.

The first story tells of the cure of a paralyzed man. This simple cure occasions conflict. Mark takes the story and shows how the healing is intended to bring out the power of forgiveness and acceptance that belongs to Jesus. As a story then there is an interaction between different groups. There is the paralyzed man, the four assistants who help him and will not be frustrated in their attempts to bring him to Jesus, the healing, forgiving and receiving power of Jesus himself, which we might call the affirming center, and finally the suspicious, jealous stance of those who are the opponents. There is a tension between the Pharisees' "questioning" and Jesus' action. This tension is between past and future, between freedom and bondage, between law and legalism, between paralysis and movement, between being for and against. It is a tension that is, it seems to me, at the heart of the story. The action that Jesus performs is obviously a healing action. Nevertheless it is viewed with suspicion. Let us move into seeing this as a story of the self.

The story calls me to identify these aspects of me. What is paralyzed? What is it in me that is not fully functioning, that is not integrated? Where is it that I sense that I am being blocked from life, from expression? Something in me is living on the periphery, on the fringe. It needs to be in touch with the deeper center where alone it can be freed and healed. Perhaps it is manifesting itself in a physical symptom, or in a pattern of inaction. So frequently I do not wish to listen to the symptoms of my life—e.g., depression, anxiety, paralysis, sexual difficulties, etc. Sometimes I do not know how to listen to them. Either way, in avoiding the symptom I am missing the message. As I return to the story I notice that the sick man is not alone. There are others.

There are helps available, there is good will. The paralyzed man has four assistants. What are these strengths in my personality? Some clues are given. They are not easily discouraged when the crowd blocks them in; they find another way. They are resourceful and determined. They are capable of enduring hardship and opposition.

Two forces of opposition are encountered in the story. One of them is the crowd who act as opposition to the four aides and the paralyzed man by their sheer presence. The presence of the crowd makes the journey to Jesus seem impossible. It will be so hard, so difficult to get through, that they will never make it because of the crowd who are also all there to see Jesus. There is so much wrong, so many things wrong, a crowd of things. That sounds familiar. I can begin to identify that attitude in me. The second force of opposition is that the story seems more directed against Jesus, against the self. It comes from suspiciousness, and it acts first of all in a questioning manner and only after the cure in a more active manner. It's an expert at justifying itself, in the name of the law, tradition, history, etc. The healing is perceived by them as loss. They lose self-esteem or power or presence or something. Theirs is the silent judgment that is heard everywhere. Every psychologist is familiar with how we tend to act against our own healing. There is a factor which they refer to as secondary gain. The patient gets something out of his sickness which at times he is unwilling or finds difficult to relinquish. Perhaps then I need here to discover what I am getting out of my paralysis. Whatever that is may view with suspicion my healing, my drawing near to the center.

In the story they find their way to Jesus by going through the roof. The roof of the person is the head which throughout time has been seen as a symbol of consciousness. Even our language speaks of "getting my head on straight," "getting my head together," etc. Something then in me needs to be brought to the roof, to consciousness. When this happens a new freedom is evidenced, and this is so pronounced that it brings forth awe and praise. Finally a reunion with the community is effected. The story in this way opens me up to growth. It surprises me. Sam Keen puts it well when he says that "awareness of what presents itself to me involves a double movement of attention, silencing the familiar and welcoming the strange. . . . If I am to appreciate the uniqueness of any datum I must be suffi-ciently aware of my preconceived ideas and characteristic emotional distortions to bracket them long enough to wel-come strangeness and novelty into my perceptual world."[4] The story thus opens me to me.

The second story in this group of conflict stories is given as the call of Levi. This story happens around a lake-shore, and again there is the presence of a crowd which are still somewhat of a collective entity, a kind of anonymous mass, but now they are undergoing instruction. Given this dimension the lakeshore is a rather appropriate place stand-ing as it does, together with water, sea, etc., as a symbol frequently used in mythology for the unconscious. In the story Levi is called to follow Jesus. He is not one of the great characters of the Gospels. In fact he is what Rhoads and Michie would call a "minor character who makes brief cameo appearances and then disappears, yet the role of each is memorable. . . . They are flat characters."[5] Levi is like that in the story. In many ways factors of life, heredity, environment and circumstances limited his choices. His work puts him into an awkward position. He is cut off from the awareness of self-worth. Clearly he functions in the story as a scapegoat for the community who can heap upon him all their hatred and unacceptable feelings. His position in the story is one of isolation. He contrasts sharply with "the crowd of on-lookers," with the large numbers who followed Jesus with the grouping of scribes and Pharisees. Everyone in the story is in a group, belongs somewhere, except Levi who stands alone and apart. The story calls me to identify that side of me. What part of me is influenced by hereditary culture, work, background ethnicity, etc., is cut off and becomes the scapegoat for the rest of men—for example, "Well, that's the drunken Irish in me," That's the demonstrative Italian in me," That's the Scot in me," etc.

The tax collectors and sinners sit with Jesus at table. Table fellowship was a sign and pledge of intimacy. There is an acceptance by Jesus of these people at the table, and even more than acceptance, there is an invitation to intimacy, to a sharing and caring for each other, to a giving of space to each other. We will see this grow in and through the feeding stories in the Gospel. These stories of Jesus' feeding, or eating with people play an important part in the Gospel. In fact there is a discernible growth as Jesus moves from the beginning where he eats with sinners outside the law, to eating with disciples in opposition to the law, to eating with disciples who are busily engaged in trying to get food for the crowd, to eating with the disciples and the crowd, to eating eventually the religious meal with the disciples. Nevertheless all these meals, even though they reflect a growing intimacy, also contain conflict of one kind or another. There is the conflict with the forces of opposition in 2:3, with the forces of discipleship in 6:8, with the forces of betrayal in Chapter 14.

This story draws attention to the tax collectors and sinners. Who are they? The textual difficulties involved in interpreting these groups are many, but what seems clear is that they are "different." Nineham indicates that the tax collectors had "a bad reputation everywhere at the time, for their dishonesty and petty extortion. . . . The sinners [could have been] the people of the land, those who had not the opportunity or inclination to study the law and carry it out in detail as the Pharisees did."[6] One wonders what does that correspond to in my personality. Is it instinct, impulse, feeling? Some part that has been looked down upon because it belongs to the earth instead of "study" (intellect)? Is this a part of me I consider valueless because of the judgment of others, because of upbringing, because of one reason or another? When or where or do I ever react emotionally? Do I feel emotion? Can I express it? If we are allowing some other aspect of ourselves to stop our emotional life, then will we be ostracized also? We are of the earth, the warm earth. We are people of the land.

Who are the Pharisees and scribes in this story? They represent the past, the law, the tradition. They are the so-called enlightened ones who are familiar with the law, etc. They represent a collective viewpoint; theirs is the stance that maintains the value of the community. They enter into conflict with Jesus about Levi, about the outcasts and sinners, about his eating with them. They seem to suggest in the story that he should not make decisions for himself, that he should not violate the law, that he should not depart from tradition, that he should not be different from them. Does this correspond to something in me wherein I permit my identification with collective values to pass judgment on myself as well? For example, I feel angry, but I deny the anger as being unacceptable, and condemn myself for feeling the anger. Is my self-worth and value then evaluated in light of what the collective perceives to be acceptable emotions? Is this in me somehow the arena of "should"?

Finally the story focuses on Jesus. This too is part of me. He receives the sinners. In fact in the story he is their guest. It is they who invite him to come, to enter into intimacy with them. He, by his acceptance, indicates his willingness to have fellowship with them. He lends them his healing power, he covers them with his intimacy, and he opposes the "party" attempt to dislodge either the sinners or himself. Schweizer makes the interesting observation regarding the "righteous" that "theirs is a temptation to think that they do not need God day by day. As a result they may not recognize God even when he comes. The danger which threatens the righteous, though it is not the same as that which threatens the outcasts, may cut them off from the living God just as effectively."[7] Jesus does not allow the expectations, or demands, or assumptions of the others in the story to define his existence or his response. He calls Levi. He treats him like a person. He speaks to him and acknowledges his existence. He enters into dialogue with him. He accepts the invitation to enter the arena and table of the outcasts. He brings all of them into the ambiance of his own life. He makes room for them as well as for the Pharisees and the Sadducees. He gives them both place and space. He brings Levi from the objective and impersonal level where he can be related to rather than dealt with, where he is mystery rather than problem. In this regard the principle of Robert Assagoli comes back to my mind: "We are dominated by everything with which our self is identified. We can dominate and control everything from which we disidentify ourselves."[8] Jesus is greater than either Levi, or the outcasts, or the Pharisees. He is that which calls to freedom and wholeness. The self that I am is greater than any of the judgments, and immensely greater than any of the punishments, and infinitely capable of transcending any limitations, and so it speaks in the middle of conflict, always inviting me into wholeness, beyond impersonalism and into freedom. Come. Follow.

The third story we have already indicated is from a number of points of view the key story in this concentric pattern of conflict stories. In this story we are once again presented with an interesting set of characters which will help and guide our meditation. Especially significant here is the dialogue about John's and Jesus' disciples. This interchange takes place between Jesus and the people. In the story people come to Jesus and ask him why the disciples of John and the Pharisees fast but his disciples do not. He answers by telling them that his disciples do not fast while the bridegroom is still present among them. Fasting was a time-honored tradition among the Jews. The Old Testament is full of events in which fasting played an important role. Sometimes it was used as an expression of sorrow for sins that had been committed. On occasion it reflected the attitude of an individual, but more frequently it reflected the sentiment of the people as a whole. It was meant to be a help to people to celebrate life. It pointed one toward life. Now however it seemed to have lost this power; the ritual had become a habit. The question posed to Jesus indicates that it was not so much the fasting as the freedom of the disciples and Jesus that was in question.

Jesus understands the direction and intent of the question. The text nowhere says that Jesus himself does not fast, and Jesus does not respond at that level. He points toward something deeper and indicates that the key issue is his presence among them. He is with them, and that is a source of joy. He is among them as the very manifestation of God's love, and therefore the appropriate response is rejoicing. Being with them, their fellowship together, their intimacy, their comradeship is what's important. They are to celebrate that event and they are to do it now.

What then is this pointing to in terms of a story of the self? Who are the disciples of John in me? What is it in me that is always preparing for the Kingdom, always procrastinating, always getting ready for tomorrow? Is there a side of me that is inappropriately fasting, holding back from play, from celebration and spontaneity until tomorrow? What is it in me that is always waiting for the perfect moment, the absolute certainty, the guaranteed result before I act? It is not that waiting is wrong, that fasting is not right, but that fasting for the sake of fasting is of little value. In waiting for perfection we miss celebrating that which is now. The self that I am is both origin and end, alpha and omega, always present in fullness and always drawing to fullness. Between the beginning and the end there is the unfolding that is the path of individuation. The self that I am is always with me, present beneath the surface changes. At the center I am in the divine image; at the center God is in me. At the center I am at once everything because I have been given all and nothing because I am nothing that I have not received. At the center I am gift, and that calls forth appreciation, thanksgiving and celebration. It is the giftedness that is to be celebrated, it is the Kingdom, it is the new wine that ever needs new skins. When the bridegroom is present it is time for feasting; when the bridegroom is absent it is time for fasting.

The story calls me then to feast and celebrate and delight in the self that I am, and in the self that I am becoming. Without this constant delighting in the self that I am, in the gift that is given, without this constant centering it will not be possible to last through conflict. At the center of conflict there is calm like the calmness at the center of a storm. The need for certainty, and desire for peace at any price, the manipulation born of the hunger for perfection are deeply imbedded in me. They can sweep me away unless I remember that at the center is the bridegroom. The central thrust must be to rejoice in the bridegroom who is always present.

The fourth conflict story again shows us Jesus present with his disciples. They are walking through a field of standing grain. As they move through the field the disciples are observed picking the grain, which causes the Pharisees to object that they are violating the sabbath. Once again the scene invokes an atmosphere of intimacy between Jesus and the disciples. They are present in the open and free atmosphere of a meadow. The fact that the grain is standing is underscored, since it indicates that the plucking of grain could then be seen as work. The apostles and Jesus are not condemned for walking in the meadow, or for admiring it, or for smelling it, etc. It is specifically the fact that they worked, that they "picked" or "plucked" the grain that is causing the conflict.

The story portrays for us a group of opponents. We have met them before in the other stories. Here again they exhibit a critical, questioning, and suspicious attitude. Once again their questioning exhibits more than a request for information. There is implicit in the question a note of both accusation and disapproval. The consistency with which Mark points out the conflicts, the constant reoccurrence of them through the Gospel, clues us to the fact that this battle is not easily won. The conflict is fought out in many ways, over many issues, and on many occasions. Nevertheless there is really only one issue, and that is the authority of Jesus. Wherever they start, whatever the initial impetus, the story returns to this each time.

Here the story begins with an observation. The disciples are "picking" grain. Nowhere does it say that Jesus himself is involved in this. Nevertheless it is Jesus who is confronted in the questioning. Work itself is not the issue, as can be seen in the response of Jesus. He shows how David felt free to break the law in the days of Abijah the high priest by entering the temple with his men and eating the holy bread. This now clearly places the conflict as one of authority. To Jesus obviously the law is a gift. It is not meant to keep man in bondage but to bring him to freedom. He feels free to go beyond the law, or rather through it. He presumes the right to interpret the law and to act upon his interpretation. He presumes to act on conscience, and it is this more than anything else that generates the hostility and suspicion of his opponents.

In terms of a story of the self then, we need to discover who the opponents are in me. What do they correspond to within me? In the story we notice that the Pharisees' life-long protective barriers are in place. They are well entrenched and rooted. They are people who are affiliated with some religious group. On the other hand they fear life and are unable to receive it except in carefully measured and articulated ways. They do not yet realize that they are in charge of their own destiny. Their affinity to the law has been shaped by their personal history, and in this form their authority has become pathological. It has been surrendered. They still look to outside events for direction and for answers. The very law which could have been of some assistance to them is now used to keep them from the life that confronts them. Perhaps this group is more than anything else a group of blamers. Virginia Satir calls blamers dictators and bosses who act superior and throw their weight around, but who are really afraid of any true discovery about themselves.[9] As I look at them they touch a chord in me. They confront me with a side of my life I don't feel very comfortable with most of the time. I become aware of how frequently I begin sentences with the accusatory and hostile "you" rather than the revealing and vulnerable "I".

Jesus on the other hand acts responsibly even if unorthodoxly. His inability and freedom as he moves through the youthful and life-giving grainfields contrasts sharply with the kind of heavy fatalism of his opponents. He is filled with love and concern for the hunger of his disciples, the isolation of outcasts, the pain of paralytics, the cause of justice, etc., and this does not appear to be the dominant concern of his opponents. There is a pronounced concern on his part as being concerned about others. Perhaps that too is part of me. At the center there is a genuine caring about people. The self is, as Jung says, an archetype of wholeness in the personality.[10] Jesus acts not so as to negate his opponents but to draw them too into the Kingdom. The self despises nothing in the personality but seeks to draw all into its freedom.

In the fifth and final story of this cycle we meet Jesus and a man with a withered hand. They come together in the synagogue on the sabbath. In the presence of the assembled congregation Jesus heals the man's hand. This provokes the Pharisees into a conscious choice, and now they leave the synagogue and plot his death. The story has a heightened sense of urgency. It is reflected in the watchfulness of the opponents from the beginning and in the switching of the initiative to Jesus. In all the other stories he is the responder; here he takes the lead in confrontation. There is an urgency also about the opponents' action, and this is reflected in the joining of forces between the Pharisees and the Herodians and in the conscious choice they make at the end of the story to plot his death.

The story is underscoring the sacredness of the whole encounter. It takes place on a sacred day in the place set aside for sacred ceremonies. It involves both the symbols of the law which is sacred, the Pharisees, and the symbol of freedom, Jesus. The hand that is cured is itself a sacred creation. The story then centers on life as sacred and as that which is in need of reverencing and healing. Life itself is to be respected and cared for, and this takes precedence over the law or anything else. Chardin in a meditation on Christ's surrendering himself into the Father's hands suggests something of the sacredness of hands when he says:

> To the hands that broke and gave life to bread,
> That blessed and caressed
> That were pierced
> To the hands that are as our hands. . . .
> To the kindly and mighty hands
>   that reach the very marrow of the soul—
>   that mold and create
> To the hands through which so great
>   a love is transmitted
> It is to these that it is good to surrender.[11]

Hands suggest possibilities that help to clarify the sacredness that is withered and deformed and somehow in need of healing. The power to touch and bless and hold, the power to stroke and support and strengthen, the power to open and to close in vulnerability, is atrophying, and Jesus moves to heal this hand.

The suspiciousness of the Pharisees gives way to plotting, to secrecy, to an association and an alliance with the forces of death. There is the glaring contrast between the forces of healing and affirmation as reflected in Jesus and the forces of suspicion and doubt mediated through the Pharisees. Maryellen Muckenhirn points out that "restless desire, not presence, presides over the time of curiosity"[12] and that is in evidence here. From the beginning their curiosity, their vigilance, their watchfulness has been creating a growing restlessness in the Pharisees. They can no longer contain it. It breaks through in a burst of secretive fury that is observable to everyone else, if not to themselves. As a story of self this is pointing toward a side of me that is curious, restless, plotting, planning, always vigilant. It focuses in on the underpinnings of my own jealousy and desires. it exposes the elements of both narcissism and voyeurism in me.

Jesus on the other hand responds. He initiates the move to wholeness, and he does so with a drive that challenges. He asks: What is the purpose of the past? What is the reason for the collective wisdom of the ages? What is the direction of the law? Is it meant for healing or harming? He clearly indicates by everything he does in the story that it is for healing. The story closes on the note of the Pharisees in their powerlessness banding together for destruction while there is a note of sadness in Jesus that his invitation to them has been neglected.

The five conflict stories come to a close, but it is clear that the conflict itself is not over. It will continue underground, in a hidden manner, surfacing periodically throughout the Gospel. It reaches different crescendo points, especially at the mid-point in Chapters 8, 9 and 10, and then again in a new frontal assault in the conflict stories of Chapter 12. Jung understood why power and authority would be a lifelong battle. He sees power and eros as being interrelated: "Where love reigns there is no will to power, and where the will to power is paramount, love is lacking. The one is but the shadow of the other; the man who adopts the standpoint of eros finds his compensatory opposite in the will to power and that of the man who puts the accent on power is eros."[13] This is also true in terms of a story of self. We are always meeting aspects of ourselves as we move into greater freedom, and this encountering causes great conflict. To be released from the bondage of necessary servitude it is first of all required that we be willing to meet the necessary voices of opposition within ourselves. Without meeting the Pharisees, etc., within and the power drive they put us in touch with, we cannot be in union by the center.

Chapter 7
The Crossing

In the next few chapters of Mark's Gospel we are going to see a number of boat trips as Jesus begins to branch out into new territory. These boat trips provide a basic structure and a unifying theme to the section. Jesus will bring his message to the people on the far side of the lake which is known as Gentile territory. As such it is foreign, unknown or rather different. The Gentiles had their own culture, their own way of worshiping God, their own style of living. They were conveniently viewed, therefore, under the deleterious and condemnatory judgment of pagans, idolators, and demon worshipers. It was easy and convenient to judge them as people without virtue, as propagators of immorality and vice. The section will speak of Jesus coming to them and speaking with them.

At the same time the section will speak of Jesus coming back from that land, of Jesus coming back to his homeland. He pays attention to what is happening there. He doesn't neglect the one for the other. Kelber, seeing this pattern, has commented that "Jesus passes from the known and friendly side of the lake to the unknown and unfriendly side."[1] This then constitutes the dynamic of the section. There is movement here. There is a flow of energy. The journey, as Kelber notices, "opens a new frontier and a breakthrough to a new identity. . . . It is not the logic of a break with the Jewish side and an unswerving pull to the Gentile side. Rather it is the logic that embraces both sides of the lake. The Jewish and Gentile side are sanctioned as if they both belonged to the Kingdom of God."[2]

Looking further at the construction of the section we notice another unifying and balancing technique that Mark uses. Whatever has occurred on the Jewish side of the lake will also occur on the Gentile side of the lake. The following chart then shows this balance in the first half of the Gospel:

LAKE

Jewish Side	Gentile Side
Exorcism of Demoniac 1:23	Exorcism of Demoniacs 5:1–20
Healing of Mother-in-Law 1:29–40	Healings 6:53–56
Conflict Stories re: Morality 2:1–3:7	Ritual Washings re: Morality 7:1–5
Jarius/Daughter and Woman 5:22	Syro-phoenician Woman and Daughter 7:24–30
Leper 1:40	Deaf Mute 7:32–37
Feed Five Thousand 6:34	Feed Four Thousand 8:12

LAKE

It is clear then that the Markan Jesus pays equal attention to both sides of the lake. This has many implications for theology, especially in the field of ecumenism, but it also is important in terms of seeing the Markan Gospel as a story of the self. Christ is here reconciling the opposites. Bonaventure later in Christian history will make this the centerpoint of his whole spiritual theology. He sees Christ as the alpha and omega, the beginning and end, the simple and composite. In Christ he sees the joining of the eternal and the temporal, Creator and creature, man and God, and, in Christ, he says, the way that the door opened between heaven and earth, death and life.[3] This reconciling of opposites that is at the heart of the Gospel and that is at the center of Christian spirituality is also at the center of the growing person.

We have already seen and referred to the fact that there are two sides to people, a conscious and an unconscious side. We have seen how within its space the psyche has energy or libido which does the work of personality. The movement of psychic processes depends on the principle of opposites. When we think of the psyche we can try to envision it as a space in which energy must be balanced. It's like a water bed. When you lie on it the water on either side balances. If it does not then you are in danger. You may fall off to either side and be hurt. Furthermore, whenever you move you displace water. If you go left then the displaced water goes right. Similarly Jung indicates that energy which moves from one part of the psyche will reappear in another part. When the psyche is balanced, then energy is free to flow and it moves outward in creativity. When the psyche is unbalanced, then the movement of energy is unbalanced and you fall out of bed. You regress. The free flow of energy is blocked and it gets dammed up in the unconscious. Edinger notes that the "self as the center and totality of the psyche which is able to reconcile all opposites can be considered the organ for excellence. Since it includes the totality it must be able to accept all the elements of psychic life no matter how antithetical they may be. It is this sense of acceptance of the self that gives the ego its strength and stability.''[4] As we go on our journey, then we will be able to experience both parts of the psyche as they seek equilibrium. In this section of the Gospel I believe that the journey of Jesus, as the archetype of the self, can help us negotiate that passage. The structure of the Gospel and the journey of Jesus opens us to the two sides of our personality and the journey of the self to unite them.

The boat journey begins for the Markan Jesus in the "evening" when he says to the apostles, "Let us go to the other side." The evening is a time of darkness, a time when the sun has gone down either totally or partially. It is a time of quietness and possibility between people. Not all darkness is frightening. There is the darkness that lovers cherish for the intimacy possibility that it affords, and while the revelation between them will demand vulnerability and revelation it is the possibilities for them that speaks the loudest. Neumann says, "It is not under the burning rays of the sun but in the cool reflected light of the moon, when the darkness of consciousness is at the full, that the creature process fullfills itself; the night, not the day, is the time of procreation. It wants darkness and quiet, and secrecy, muteness and hiddenness. Therefore the moon is Lord of life in opposition to the lethal devouring sun. The moist nighttime is the time of sleep, but also of healing and recovery."[5]

The journey across the lake however will not be an easy one. The boat is beset very quickly with winds and storm. These apparently were not unusual, nor are they today, on Lake Galilee. Nevertheless one gets the sense that this is an unusual kind of event. The unexpectedness of the storm, the rapidity with which it formed, the violence of its power, the strength of its onslaught—all of these are essential to the story. They are pointing toward the difficulty of the crossing, the uncertainty and risk involved, the fearsome nature of the journey, etc. Each of the other boat trips in this section also has elements of danger connected to it. Either crowds spring up or the people crowd him or they forget the food, etc. The danger is present constantly.

In the story the wind and waves are seen in relationship to one another. They begin to act in consort and in harmony, forging a conjoint attack upon the ship. The waves are sinking the ship. They sweep over the bow. The wind whips them into a fury so that the apostles are frightened. This combination of wind and water is very interesting. On their own they are symbols within Scripture with their own individual history. We meet them also on different occasions when they are paired together. In Genesis 1:2 we read how a mighty wind swept over the waters. In Exodus 14:21 we are told how Moses stretched his hand out over the sea, and the Lord swept the sea with a strong east wind throughout the night and so turned it into a dry land. In Ezekiel 36:25 we come upon the elements again when Yahweh says to the people, "I will sprinkle clean water upon you to cleanse you from all impurities, and from all your idols I will cleanse you. I will give you a new heart and plant a new spirit within you. . . . You shall live in the land I gave your fathers." Wind and water then have this interior relationship to one another. One wonders therefore if their interrelationship here is more than merely descriptive of a storm. In the passages cited they act together for a purpose. They are seen as cleansing, creating, forming. There is a creativity about their combined activity. There is something new happening. On each occasion their activity is followed by a new movement which can perhaps best be described as a movement out of chaos and into union. In Genesis it's from original chaos into life as being, life as man and woman, life as choice and consciousness. In Exodus it's from life as slavery and bondage into freedom, life as servant and taskmaster into life as chosen and cared for by another. In Ezekiel it's life out of corporate responsibility and exile into individual responsibility and intimacy. We shall meet this combination again in John 3:4 when they become the requirement for new birth: "No one can enter the Kingdom of God unless he is born of water and the spirit. A man is born physically of human parents but he is born spiritually of the spirit."

This combination of elements then which appear to be thrown together in the crossing seem to be pointing to a new moment. Wind and water announce a new birth, new possibilities, liberation from bondage, etc. The crossing is not easy. The bringing of the two sides of the lake together is difficult. The unification or balancing of the polar opposites is not easy to achieve. Nevertheless the journey is worthwhile. It contains new possibilities for the personality. Many journeys may be required but eventually new birth takes place. It must be noted also that the wind and water pose no threat for Jesus. They act so as to frighten the disciples but Jesus himself is asleep in the back of the boat. It is the disciples who fear this moment and see in it an advent of death. "Don't you care," they ask, "that we die?" Jesus by contrast is resting, sleeping. He awakens and commands the wind and water to be quiet. Something is dying, something is being born. Across the lake the opposites are being drawn into union.

Harrington points to three contrasts within the story itself: "1. the plight of the storm-tossed boat with the tranquil sleep of Jesus; 2. the abject terror of the professional fishermen with the sovereign calm of the master who commands winds and waves with authority; 3. the reaction of the disciples to Jesus."[6] In all three the center that is Jesus

holds together. The center moves onward toward the unification of Jewish and Gentile lands, the center moves to
feeding and healing and celebrating. In all three the center
exudes confidence. It is the place to be. In a later story in
the same section the disciples will again be on the water
(6:45), but on this occasion Jesus will not be with them.
Instead he comes to them walking on the water. Again
there are the winds and the waves. This time, however,
they see Jesus and they think he is a ghost. He is not with
them in the boat. He is the familiar friend. He is the Lord.
He is the one they have been with. All along they were
together. Now they mistake him for a ghost. When Jesus is
with them he is asleep; when he is absent and comes
toward them they think he is a ghost. The image in both
cases is that they are falling apart. In his poem T.S. Eliot
speaks of a point that we reach or come to in life.[7] He calls
it the "still point," a point of intersection between time and
the timeless, between stillness and movement. It is a position at the center that is markedly in contrast to the surface
movements to panic and overactivity. Without reaching this
point Eliot says that man is going to be "in a dark wood, in
a bramble, on the edge of a grimpen, where there is no
secure foothold."[8] He will be a man "in a drifting boat with
a slow leakage, the silent listening to the undeniable clamour of the bell of the last annunciation."[9] Here Jesus is the
still point sleeping in the boat or coming to them out of the
chaotic waters of the surface and leading them on to the
other side.

The story calls me to further growth. In the developing
years I am called upon to stay on one side of the lake. I
develop what Jung called the persona. I develop by typo-
logical characteristics. I develop my strengths. I become
conscious of the who that I am at a certain level. But life
brings me to a moment when I must cross the lake and

reach the other side. The lake, the sea, as we have already mentioned, is frequently a symbol of the unconscious. Better still probably is it for us to ask: What is the lake? What is the fluid substance in which I now find myself? What is it like to be in a boat? What is it like when the familiarity of the boat and the security of the boat are threatened? What is it like when the storm rises and the winds blow and the water starts to come aboard? What is the wind and water in my life that threatens the boat? What is the boat in me, the familiar security, the thing I have known the most? What is it like to feel this sudden unpreparedness for onslaught? Where is the center? Where is the self? Where is the Jesus center? Can I believe there is a birth happening in the middle of all of this? Is it birth or death or both or neither? T.S. Eliot put it like this in "Journey Of The Magi":

> . . . were we led all that way for
> Birth or Death? There was a Birth, certainly,
> We had evidence and no doubt. I had seen birth and
>   death,
> But had thought they were different; this Birth was
> Hard and bitter agony for us, like Death, our death.[10]

In the crossing the opposites are reconciled and drawn together but the crossing is not easy. It is difficult and sometimes feels and looks more like death than birth, but then maybe these two are opposites that are reconciled in the journey to the center of the self.

Chapter 8
The Shadow

Throughout these few chapters we see Jesus crossing the lake and bringing both sides into union. This crossing of the lake, we see, is filled with difficulty, sea storms, etc. We viewed it then in terms of two sides of the personality, and the deeper striving under the impetus of the self for a new union. Jolande Jacobi points out that there can be "a rebirth of the suppressed unlived nature in man as well as a rebirth of the neglected and undeveloped spirit, both of which must be sought in order to round out the individual into a whole."[1] The rebirth she is speaking of affects the whole person, but, as she is clear to indicate, it does so in stages. "Rebirth can only proceed step by step affecting the individual first in one part and then in another until it finally encompasses the whole life."[2]

Rebirth then is ongoing and it is deepening. It follows more the pattern of a spiral than of any linear progression. There is a development but it does not follow any chronological order. We go over things as if we were repeating the same path and yet it is not exactly the same. Things overlap each other as we advance. We see this in the story of the

Gerasenes in Chapter 5 of the Gospel. At first it appears to be merely a repeat of the story of the demoniac as we witnessed in Mark 2. This story, however, happens on the other side of the lake. That as we have seen makes it more significant. Is it merely repeating on one side of the lake what took place on the other? No, there is new birth. In Jesus the two sides are bridged. The story itself of the man living in the land of Gedara is more fleshed out, more concrete, more detailed and more real in a sense.

All of us in the course of our living develop, as we have seen, a mask, a kind of facade that Jung called the persona. This facade plays an important part in our life. It helps us to adapt to our environment. It is the outer garment that we can cloak ourselves in as we present ourselves to the world. It aids us in our development of a style of life, facilitates us in our project of living and renders us socially acceptable. The underside of the persona is the shadow. The more one becomes identified with the persona the stronger will become the shadow. They are compensatory. The brighter the outer light, the shining social side, the darker will be the hidden shadow. Much of our personality then lies hidden in the shadows. If this were not so then our lives would be like a Hollywood set, all frontage with nothing behind, easily destroyed and torn down.

The shadow is unconscious, that is, it lies beneath the surface. In the course of our own growth and development all of us find that there are certain impulses, feelings, tendencies that are unacceptable in our lives. Generally we are not aware of these precisely because they are unacceptable. We have however devised a way in the course of living for getting rid of them. We banish them from our lives. This enables us to live in the glorious innocence of the first naiveté. However we soon come to discover that what we had banished never really left. It was merely hidden and lived its own life from the depths. Since we did not own these "unacceptable" impulses they tended to own us. They must then be reclaimed if growth is to occur.

It is important to recognize that the "shadow," as Jung called this grouping of characteristics that is not acceptable to the conscious self, is not always negative. It is true that it is mostly the inferior characteristics that are relegated to the shadow. In many cases, however, positive potentialities are also dormant, as far as consciousness is concerned, in the shadow. The effect of the shadow is to permit an individual to hate and judge, to condemn and villify others while maintaining a sense of his own righteousness. In fact there is a compensatory relationship between the two. The bigger the shadow, the greater the sense of righteousness. This enables us to understand how sometimes our greatest virtues turn out to be our largest vices and conversely sometimes what we think are our biggest sins and vices turn out to be assets and gems seeking expression through our life.

The shadow has its own manner of operation. The energy consigned to the shadow may be hidden and repressed but it is not dead. The contents are entombed but not destroyed. They are still alive even though dissatisfied with the current level of existence. They do not like being unacknowledged and seek expression. Since they are unacceptable to the conscious mind they are catapulted outward toward whatever is present in the environment. This catapulting activity is called by Jung projection. All the unacceptable impulses then are piled into the object of our projection and then the interior conflict is resolved or so it appears. The shadow is "transferred to the outside world and is experienced as an outside object."[3]

Since the shadow now exists outside of us in our projection, it is correct to say that we encounter our shadow. We run into it and meet it in the most unusual and, to us, surprising places. The cultivated blindness that has allowed us to function is suddenly being shattered. Generally a good key to a shadow meeting is this kind of shattering. We begin to feel uncomfortable, tense, unusually annoyed, etc. The key then is in our affective response to a stimulus that we meet. We will find ourselves, to paraphrase Neumann, more interested in not looking, in overlooking, or in looking the other way than in sharpening our senses of observation.[4]

What is the value of noting our affective responses to things and events if they merely hint at the existence and presence of a shadow content? The value lies in confronting the projection and withdrawing it, in bringing the projected content home. In this way the darkness in ourselves is illuminated and made conscious. The ego is deflated or brought back to size. It is enabled to let go of its illusions about itself and then empowered to live a little more fully in the world of reality. We soon discover that our ideals have frequently been only disguised advances for power, our sacred convictions so often only subtle attempts to reinforce our own position, etc. The shadow figure comes as a messenger of the unconscious inviting us to pay attention to something bigger then our own little ego concerns. The shadow leads us to ourselves, to the deeper self, if we listen attentively.

Let us return then to the story. Jesus as we saw crosses the lake and begins there to do what he had done previously in Jewish territory. Kelber notes that to fully understand the exorcism that now takes place we must briefly flash back to an event in the first half of the Gospel. "Immediately following the call of the four disciples Jesus had performed an exorcism in the synagogue at Capernaum as his first public act. . . . Jesus opened his public activity with an exorcism in a Jewish setting. After the breakthrough toward the Gentiles on the eastern side of the lake he does exactly what he had done on the Jewish side—he performs an exorcism."[5]

First let us look at the territory that he arrived in on the eastern side of the lake. Mark calls it the territory of the Gerasenes which is clearly a pagan town even though its exact whereabouts are unknown.[6] This is an unknown and unfriendly land. It is the pagan land, the darkness which, with the coming of Jesus, is now being illuminated and invited into the Kingdom of God. The light of Christ is reaching out to the Gentiles to embrace them also within the Kingdom. They too are to hear the good news. This, says Nineham, is the "first time in the Gospel that Jesus has been in Gentile territory, so it is more noteworthy that his holy presence routs and banishes uncleanness."[7] This land then is clearly from a Jewish perspective the dark unfriendly unconverted side. This is further borne out by the description of the man that he meets there when he lands. We immediately notice all the dark and heavy qualities that are descriptive of him. According to the Scripture, "he was a man from the tombs, who lived among the graves, who was restrained and bound, who was no longer able to be controlled, whose breaking loose endangered his own life and that of everyone else, who was constantly, night and day, howling and gashing himself in a self-destructive manner.

The words of description clearly signify the potentiality for anger, hatred, destruction, etc. Mark pays particular attention here to a description of the body involvement, as if it is a clue to the problem, and yet he clearly indicates it is not the problem, only the manifest. The problem itself is much deeper. There is a deeper conflict, an inner struggle. The inner demon is pleading to be freed, to be released, and somehow it sees Christ as the answer to the conflict.

The pattern of the dialogue follows the earlier pattern of Chapter 2. There is first of all a battle for naming, for control. Jesus asks clearly, "What is your name?" and the demon surrenders his name to Jesus. He is Legion, a name that translates as "mob." He is multiple, then, or many-faceted. Secondly we notice that initially the man wants to hold on to the drives that control his life. He wants to hang on to them, if not within his own person, at least within the ambiance of the world he knows. "Don't send them out of the territory" is the appeal he makes to Jesus. The presence of the pigs is convenient for Mark's purpose in the story, but perhaps there is more here than we are inclined to think of right away. Schweizer sees in their presence in the story evidence of a Jewish storyteller for whom the "pigs are a very desirable dwelling place"[8] for the demons.

In mythology pigs are an important animal. Their consistent presence in different cultural mythologies seems to indicate that we may be dealing with something that is part of the collective experience of mankind. Pigs are used with remarkable consistency in different cultures and times for similar kinds of expression of meaning. Joseph Campbell in his great work on mythology traces their presence in different cultures and even indicates how through a comparative study one can trace the evolutionary strain of mankind. He shows how in such stories as Tuwale in West Ceram, Persephone in Greek mythology, Diarmuid and Grainne in Irish folklore, etc., the sacrificial pig has great significance in terms of birth and death, departure, initiation and return. It relates to the great themes and frames the high moments of the merging of the two worlds of Eternity and Time, death and life, father and son.[9] In the reference to pigs then, perhaps we are touching upon the collective unconscious that Jung speaks of in his writings. It may indicate what he calls a "big dream," but we shall leave the consideration of that for another time. Notice however what happens to the demons. First, they were named; second, they were claimed (the man comes to Jesus and acknowledges his condition). They are now projected outward onto the pigs, the convenient scapegoats where their destructive quality becomes visible. The pigs run and jump over the cliff. The shadow when it is projected is dangerous and destructive.

Notice that the "herdsmen fled." They "ran off and brought the news to field and village, and people came out to see what had happened." The freed man is liberated, and initially this means a new loneliness. Everybody deserts him even if for good reason. This loneliness at the end of the story however is in marked contrast to the tomb-like loneliness at the beginning. There are, it seems, two kinds of loneliness, that at the top of the totem pole and that at the bottom. The one I call decision loneliness (top), the other I call desperation loneliness. This man is freed from the latter for the former. He is freed for leadership, and it is on this note that the story concludes. The man "went away and began to proclaim throughout the ten cities what Jesus had done for him. They were all amazed at what they heard." This is the final relief. The man is freed, the energies that had previously been blocked are liberated, the energy that was being utilized to keep the demons in check are now turned to other uses. The man is now able from within himself to redirect his energy, to better utilize his time, to expand his space and to enlarge his vision.

As we revisit this story then in terms of a story of the self, our eyes are drawn to the revelatory aspects of the body, to the projective practices of our life, to the need for sacrifice and the possibilities of birth engendered in encountering the shadow. The Christ center is crossing the lake of our life inviting us to a new integration, to a new freedom in and through the discovery of the demons that control our existence. The clue to the existence of the shadow is twofold: (1) the body in our life and (2) the pigs in our life.

Arthur Vogel correctly states that our bodies reflect our style of life, our project of existence.[10] We know even more of this from the study of psychosomatic medicine.[11] The body is a statement. It is revelatory of the kind of ordered or disordered existence we are leading. It tells us of our drivenness, our compulsiveness, our destructiveness, our anxiety, etc. It speaks to us of our thirst for pleasure, hunger, pain, childhood, etc. So I return to look at my body. Am I overweight or underweight? What foods am I eating? Is it a balanced diet? Am I exercising or out of breath with mild exercise? Am I drinking too much or taking drugs and chemicals to sleep, to wake up, to drown out the past or the future? Have I had a check-up recently? Is my blood pressure up or down? Etc., etc. I look at my body, and it reveals to me some of the shadow, the hidden project of existence that is going on in my life.

In the story Christ, the self center in our personal story, is pushing for something more. He is calling the man into wholeness, integrity, inviting him into the Kingdom of light. He is speaking to the spoken and unspoken but expressive desire of the man for wholeness. Carl Braaten says that "every sick person is crying out for a double diagnosis, first a medical diagnosis of the organ in trouble, and second an interpretation of the person as a whole, how he lives and what he eats, how he sleeps and recreates, how he works and exercises, how he prays and what he dreams of, his sex and family life, his hates and loves, his fears and hopes."[12] In the Gospel story as in our story the unacceptable, yet clearly living, impulses in the man are distorted. His bodily presence gives him the appearance of one from the caves, the graves, the tombs. I need to see and feel, and accept the statement that my body is making. Is my body reflecting my conscious life project or is it saying something else that I do not wish to hear but need to hear?

Second I need to discover the "pigs" in my life. The pet names and spiteful names I have for others will frequently help me in this regard. The strength of the affect I have toward others will help. The unacceptable impulses are projected onto others. My relationship with others can tell me more about myself than anyone else. They provide me with important data about myself. I need to become aware of the appropriateness of my feelings. Those feelings are appropriate which help to bring about a greater sense of integrity and unity within the person. Those feelings are inappropriate that are self-defeating, self-sabotaging and destructive. The affect is out of balance with the injury or cause, etc. In this manner I can begin to become aware of the voice of the shadow. They reflect back to me what I cannot see about myself. They speak to me of my hidden agendas, my unconscious ideals, my secret longings, my manipulations, etc.

The pigs in my life are indeed all the unacceptable negatives in my life. However "my own shadow side is a part and a representative of the shadow side of the whole human race; and if my shadow is anti-social and greedy, cruel and malicious, poor and miserable—if he approaches me in the form of a beggar, a negro or a wild beast—then my reconciliation with him will involve at the same time my reconciliation with the dark brother of the whole human race. This means that when I accept him and, in him, myself, I am also accepting, in his person, the whole component of the human race which—as my shadow—is my neighbor."[13] Frequently it is by putting others down that I make myself feel good, or by making others feel badly that I make myself feel better, etc. How frequently as I look to my life I find that others are the guilty victims and I am the innocent accuser. Events like these open me to the pigs in my life, to the shadow. Under the guidance of the self we are called to recognize the shadow and bring it into the light, to integrate its energies, its values, its strength into our personality, to bring them into our conscious mode of operation and grow into the person we are called to become.

Chapter 9
The Feminine

In the general section that we have been considering we have watched Jesus cross the lake in an attempt to unite both sides within the Kingdom. Part of that attempt as Mark sees it involves women. Jesus meets them on both sides of the lake. We have only encountered one woman in the Gospel so far, and that was on that "typical day" that Mark described.[1] Now, however, in rapid succession there are four stories involving women. Even the very number four, as we outline them, strikes one immediately as interesting:

1. Story of Jairus and his daughter 5:21 (Jewish)
2. Story of hemorrhaging woman 5:25 (Jewish)
3. Story of Herod, his wife and daughter 6:4 (pagan)
4. Story of Syro-phoenician woman 7:24 (pagan)

Quickly observing these stories we notice immediately the balance between Jewish and pagan women. There are two stories relating to each. We also have commented previously on how the trip across the lake begins on the Jewish side and terminates in Gentile territory. During this series

81

of stories then Jesus will have extended the Kingdom geographically, ethnically and sexually.[2]

The journey has implications for a story of the self. In
the last chapter we spoke of the shadow figure as the bearer
of our projected unacceptable impulses. The shadow figure
is usually of the same sex as the person who has projected
their inferior parts onto them. There is however another
kind of projection that occurs. In every age and in every
culture certain characteristics and qualities tend to be associated with men and certain characteristics with women.
Some characteristics are appropriate to both but, for whatever reason, some characteristics are seen to be inappropriate to one group or another—e.g., in some cultures men
are not supposed to be weak, which frequently translates
as: they are not to cry; in some cultures women are supposed to be obedient, which translates as: they are not to
think. In both groupings then we have a whole series of
qualities which are excluded from consciousness. These
repressed or hidden qualities gather around what Jung
called the "contrasexual image" which means they gather
round a feminine image in the psyche of a man and the
masculine image in the psyche of a woman. This second
figure generally appears once the shadow figure has been
integrated into consciousness and it brings with it new and
different problems.[3] The appearance of this new figure her-
alds a new moment of growth and advance. It is in this view
then that I want to try to approach the four figures or stories
mentioned above.

Looking over the four stories I notice that they have a
number of things in common. These I describe as follows:

1. A pattern of woundedness. In each of the four stories
   there is an element of woundedness or pain and it is, by
   and large, mediated through the woman in the story. In

the story of Jairus it is his daughter. Her pain is not peripheral or incidental. It is the thing that motivates and energizes Jairus to go searching for the healer. In the second story the woundedness is reflected in the flow of blood which embarrasses the woman so deeply that her life is presented in a furtive manner. She pursues her healing from a position hidden within the crowd. In the third story there is a lot of pain, and many wounds. There is Herod's inability to relate to anyone on a personal level. He has clearly become isolated. His relationship to John the Baptist is based on fear, his relationship to his wife is contaminated by jealousy, his relationship to the crowd is framed by his desire, and his relationship to Salome is in turn colored by the presence of his guests. Herod is a pleaser on many levels masquerading as a tyrant. He is a man without interiority or substance. Hence one sees Herodias' woundedness. She is cut off, she is distanced, distracted from the possibility of intimacy. She is however both Herod's hope and despair. His inability to reach his wife is in turn explored and exploited by Salome. This family is a family that triangulates in pain. In the final story it is again the woundedness of a child, a daughter, that catalyzes the mother to search for the healer. Each of the stories then portrays a wounded woman waiting in a kind of prison to be liberated and in each story there is a liberation. The daughter of Jairus is revivified, the woman with the hemorrhage is healed, the demon leaves the daughter of the Syro-phoenician woman. What about Herodias? Here there is no record of healing, but it is notable also that Jesus is absent.

2. Each story has an element of surprise. In the story of the daughter of Jairus for instance you expect her to be dead

when you finally get to the house. Everything points in that direction—the weeping and wailing, the arrival of the messengers, etc. Just when you're ready to accept that, the surprise comes and you discover that she is raised. In the second story there is a double surprise. First there is the surprise in discovering that this woman expects to be healed without being touched, or examined, or noticed, or even mentioning her pain. The bigger surprise comes, however, when she is healed. Jesus not only stops and notices her existence but goes beyond that and calls her forth from the group. He deliberately brings her from the background to the foreground, and when the apparent austerity of his remark, "Who touched me?" might lead you to think that he was going to be stern and authoritarian with whoever had touched his garment, you again get surprised. There is no condemnation, no punishment, only acceptance. He does not try to demean her or embarrass her, but rather he accepts, acknowledges and appreciates her. In the story of Herod the surprise comes when he discovers Salome's request. It jumps out at you the way Herodias and Salome have conspired together to trap the king. The pleasure of the banquet and the ability to continue as king can now only continue with violence and destruction to something essential. Herod, in publicly acknowledging Salome's presence and request, must now either kill John the Baptist which he would prefer not to do, or back down in front of his guests which he can't afford to do. There is a surprise then in seeing that the king's freedom is all a facade. He has no interiority. He is a man without inner power. In the fourth story the surprise comes with the discovery of the strength and persistency of the woman. You do not expect this. Her position and presence are clearly meant to be inconsequential. She has no right to be heard. She has two strikes against her. She is a woman and she is a foreigner, neither of which had much standing in the Jewish world.[4] But then comes the double surprise. She not only approaches Jesus and takes the initiative, she not only speaks, but she persists, and demands to be given a hearing. You find persistency and resiliency where you do not expect to find it. Finally there is a further surprise in that no healing of the girl is mentioned even though it is clearly implied.

3. The element of hiddenness is common to all the stories. In each of the events one of the key components is hidden, is in the background somewhere; it is just alluded to in some fashion. Nevertheless this hiddenness which in each of the stories is connected with woman is essential to the story and its unfolding. In the Jairus story the daughter is the hidden presence. She never really emerges as a strong figure in the story, and yet her presence dominates the story which is really about the faith/ existence/conversion of her father. There is an implied relationship between her woundedness and his panic, her apparent death and his search for life, her alienation and his community, her isolation and his search for intimacy with Jesus. In the second story we see the woman with the hemorrhage approaching Jesus on the blind side. Mark says: "She heard about Jesus and so she came in the crowd behind him." The hiddenness is further alluded to in that her suffering is going for twelve years and that instead of getting better by going to all the doctors she is getting worse. The very story itself further emphasizes the hidden quality since it is a story hidden within a story. This woman is, to use a phrase of Gertrude Von Le Fort, "silent, hidden, invisible action." In the Herod sequence the plotting and conniving that exists

between Herodias and Salome is very much an aside. It's in the background. Nevertheless it dominates the scene. The whole meaning of the scene flows from this interchange. This plotting eventually exposes Herod's compulsiveness, lust, powerlessness, and greed. It is then the hidden energy that mobilizes the action of the story. Finally in the fourth story the hidden quality emerges in the child who never enters the story, and is never present to Jesus. This story is really a story about outsiders and insiders, the foreigners and the native born, the Israelites and others.

4. The faces of women are a common element in the stories. The faces reflect many dimensions, giving an element of difference within similarity to the women in the story. One cannot say that the women, as presented in Mark, stand for this or that and be content with a single explanation. In the story of Salome and Herod woman is presented as one who both lures Herod away and at the same time exposes him to himself. She infatuates him, and from the story it appears that her seduction is deliberate. She forces him into a position from which there is no escape. Nevertheless in a compensatory way her presence reveals his inability to relate to his wife, etc. She shows him to be a man living on the external trappings of existence. She then represents the instinctual with its rhythm, its dance, its biological emphasis.

A different dimension is revealed when we look at the woman with a hemorrhage. This woman is suffering from a flow of blood. In the Old Testament blood is the very thing that distinguishes the living from the dead. Even more important is the fact that blood is related to God, to Yahweh.[5] This woman represents more than merely instinctual life. The life that is being reflected here is a life that is ebbing out of us, being lost, being poured out and wasted. It is lost in inferiority, in the feeling that it can only get in through the back door. This situation of inferiority has been accepted for twelve years. There are powers that seek to keep her in the background, but she finds her way to the Lord, guided by the vision she has seen, the power she has intuited, the otherness she sensed in the rather possessive world around her.

There is a third face presented in the story of Jairus and his daughter. The girl is presented as being twelve years old, a fact which Kelber notes is a "clear signal of the Jewishness"[6] of the event. Being twelve is also important in that place and period of history since it indicates a girl of marriageable age. She is then a woman prepared for intimacy, for life, for revelation, but instead of intimacy, closeness, and friendship she is isolated cut off and alone. She is a woman in need of awakening, says Christ, and indeed she responds to his summons and his call. It is not without significance that the three apostles Peter, James, and John are present as witnesses to this episode. They are the same ones who will witness the transfiguration and the sorrow in Gethsemani. The fourth face we see reflected in the story of the Syro-phoenician woman. The woman in this story is liberating, persistent and consistent. She is assertive and not easily moved from her purpose. She is assertive without being either aggressive, defensive, or apologetic. In fact what is noticeable in this story is that it is Jesus who wants to hide. "He went into a house; he didn't want anyone to know he was there but he could not stay hidden" (7:24). This woman is an invitation to Jesus to expand his consciousness and his horizons. She uses her wit and her charm to invite him to do that, and in his manner of responding it is clear that he accepts the invitation even if it appears that he is initially

reluctant. In taking this step of consciousness expansion
he is also facilitating other steps that quickly follow when
tax collectors, a Roman centurion and others enter his
life. This encounter with the Syro-phoenician woman
impacted upon his own understanding of his mission, his
life and his future. Because of her the narrowness of his
initial vision was broadened out into a more comprehen-
sive view.[7]

The journey across the lake then in terms of the story
of the self is a journey to integration. We have seen some
of this in the meeting with the shadow. Now we touch a
new depth in terms of a meeting with the opposites. The
goal for each person's journey is psychic wholeness. The
masculine and feminine characteristics must be brought
into a relationship with each other in the personality.
According to Jung sexual differences are basic. They reflect
something essential in the human person. Neither man nor
woman is complete without absorbing some basic characteristics of the opposite sex. I say characteristics since we all
have all the characteristics, but certain ones seem to dominate in males and others in females. As I turn my eyes now
to these four figures of Scripture I become mindful that they
are reflective of figures in my inner being. They have both
positive and negative characteristics. Von Franz says that
the "negative anima in a man's personality can be revealed
in waspish, poisonous, effeminate remarks by which he
devalues everything. . . . In this guise the anima is as cold
and reckless as certain uncanny aspects of nature itself, and
in Europe is often expressed to this day by belief in
witches."[8] On the other hand she affirms the positive role
of the anima also by saying that it occurs "when a man
takes seriously the feelings, moods, expectations and fantasies sent by his anima and when he frees them in some

form, for example in writing, painting, sculpture, musical composition or dancing. . . . After a fantasy has been fixed in some specific form it must be examined both intellectually and ethically, with an evaluating feeling reaction . . . If this is practiced with devotion over a long period the process of individuation gradually becomes the single reality and can unfold in its true form."[9]

These four figures then from the Scripture speak to me in my meditation. They speak of something that is hidden in me that perhaps I have never seen before, never been aware of until now, but which if I can incorporate into my consciousness will give me greater freedom and identity. There is through these images something possibly trying to break into my life out of the collective images of my Christian heritage. It tries to break in as surprise, as suddenness, and until the breakthrough to consciousness occurs I am still wounded, broken, and divided. This something is that "problematic partner"[10] that we referred to earlier with her different faces in history. So I turn now to the four figures and see them each in turn.

The Syro-phoenician woman is the first one I notice. She puts me in touch with the mothering image as she expresses in regard to her child the protective, sheltering stance. Her presence and activity in the story, her coming to Jesus, her persistence, etc., reveals her to me as the caring mother, the seeker of life and happiness for her daughter. She is the giver of nutrition and health, and for her no walls or barriers are too difficult or too great to surmount. She plods on irrespective of the obstacles, willing to sacrifice everything if necessary for the sake of her child. She calls me by her existence in the story to identify the mother within me. This brings me back in touch with the mother I incorporated in my youth, in my childhood. She now either consciously or unconsciously colors my relationships, my emotions, my fantasies, my imaginations. She stands guard over my expectations as the Syro-phoenician woman placed her expectations, gave voice to expectations, from her relationship with Christ. Her aliveness in me is now being called to be recognized. Looking at the Syro-phoenician woman however may evoke a different mother within. I may come to see her now as the devouring mother who takes over her daughter's life, who has not nourished her and strengthened her, who has now abandoned her in her illness instead of sending someone else. She is now the mother that can be likened to the goddess of death and famine and plague who abandons the earth and is the bringer of death instead of life. This mother too may be alive in me, and the story calls me to reflect upon that and how it is present in my now relationships. The Syro-phoenician mother then in her petitioning and receiving, in her practicality and earthiness, in her strength and concern, as she deals with the reality of her situation calls forth to consciousness this hidden aspect of my life.

In the next story my eyes are caught by Salome. She is a pushy and energetic woman. She knows how to get her own way and lets nothing interfere with her goals. She is capable of using friendship or relationship, talent, plotting or intrigue to carve out for herself what she desires. She seeks only her own goals and purposes. She is not concerned about Herod's feelings, his guests, his politics, his position or his status. She is capable of calmly asking for the head of John the Baptist in the middle of a banquet without giving even a momentary consideration to the effect it has on the dinner guests. This is a view of another woman that lives within. She is cool, calm and career oriented. She can play the part of a little girl who listens to her mother but who in reality is a dangerous enemy. Underneath the exterior mask is a fire-breathing dragon who slays and destroys at will. I am called now to acknowledge her presence within me in the poisonous and venomous moods of revenge that surface before my eyes.

In the third figure that catches my attention I find another dimension. This time it is the woman with the hemorrhage. The woman within who is bleeding calls out for recognition. She too is hidden in the crowd of the unconscious. She appears to me in the story as the woman of intuition and faith who perceives the possibilities in the moment and is in tune and relatedness with what the poet calls the "deep down freshness of things." This woman sensed something fresh, something different in her relationship to Jesus. She could see to the depth of things and she trusted that; she abandoned herself to her intuition and her heart. There is here a kind of wisdom that penetrates, that goes beyond the rational and the logical and transcends it. The way in which Jesus stops and calls her forth is itself rather extraordinary. Nowhere else does he do anything like that in Scripture. He summons her from the crowd. He calls her forth, and we are required to ask "Why?" Was it to embarrass her, or confuse her, or ridicule her? Such would appear to be in glaring contrast to his profile in the rest of Scripture. It must have been to appreciate her and to affirm and confirm the gift of her intuition. Alicia Faxon hypothesizes that in confronting her Jesus was "making her stand up and be counted. . . . That he didn't treat her like a child but like a mature person."[11] This woman wanted to be connected and she moved to establish that for herself. She represents then something within that desire to be connected, related to, the someone I intuit as present. She is thus the wise woman, but indeed others might see in her a different dimension. She could be equally a figure perhaps of madness whose whole perspective is formed by a magical view of existence. She is caught by the dangerously fascinating elements which bring madness as well as wisdom. The allure of the unconscious, the entry into the religious, the meeting with the sacramental, the language of the mysteries can be a way to both wisdom and folly, and so like the other figures we have met she too has positive and negative possibilities.

The last story to speak brings forth the presence of the little girl. We have previously noted how she is a woman of marriageable age. She is then a woman ready for intimacy, for self-disclosure and for commitment to another person. Alicia Faxon calls her a young girl suffering through an "adolescent crisis." However, instead of that happening this young girl is portrayed as sick, or asleep or dying. Something is wrong. Instead of forging ahead and embracing that kind of commitment she is instead kept forever in perpetual preparedness. In her book Jean Gill sees her as an image of our inner child and then asks us to consider our own inner child. She suggests some of the following as characteristics of the child: "inquisitive, sensitive, trusting, dependent, adventurous, emotional, receptive, open, creative, playful, searching, mischievous, imaginative, growing, accepting, full of wonder and awe, curious."[12] She asks us then to consider our emotional life which if buried brings a "deadly illness upon our inner child" and she suggests the following exercise as a way toward healing the inner child: "a. write down all the emotions you can think of, b. accept yourself as capable of feeling each of them, cherish each emotion."[13] Here then we see the young girl in a death condition and her healing and restoration come with being awakened. There is thus a call to the young girl sleeping within who needs to be called forth into consciousness.

We have been looking at these figures of the inner world, these women within. James Hillman writes that "since men do live psychologically in a harem it is useful to get to know one's inner household. We do well to know by what fascination we are bewitched, turned into phallic animal, petrified into immobility, or lured underwater and away from real life. We do well to know whom we are unconsciously following in counsel, where our Cinderella sits in dirt and ashes, or Snow White lies in poisoned sleep, what hysterical feminine tricks we play deceivingly on ourselves with affects and moods, which muse inspires or Beatrice ignites, and which is the true favorite who moves the deepest possibilities of our nature and holds our fate."[14] We have looked at the stories and allowed ourselves to be guided by them to the inner woman hiding within, emerging in our lives constantly as surprise, emerging frequently as wounded and in need of attention, emerging in a multiplicity of faces. It is also true that others reading the Gospel will perhaps select other figures as guides to the man within. This however is beyond the scope of this particular reflection.[15]

Chapter 10
The Loaf

We have noted previously the unity of this section of the Gospel, from Chapter 4 to Chapter 8. Initially we saw it as a unity in terms of Jesus crossing the lake and thus uniting both sides. The lake then which initially was a barrier of separation is transformed and now becomes a symbol of unification. Then we saw a second uniting dimension in the bringing together of the forces on both sides of the lake, a movement we tried to understand in terms of light and shadow, Jew and Gentile, etc. A third moment of unity was discovered in the expansion of that idea into the area of the contrasexual opposites through reflection upon the feminine figures on both sides of the lake. Now we have a fourth symbol in this section, namely bread, or, to use the title of this chapter, "the loaf."

Stories of bread occur throughout all sections of this Gospel. There is a story of feeding in Levi's house (2:13), and of disciples eating grain (2:12), in the early portion of the Gospel. Later in the Gospel there is a story of Jesus eating with the disciples (14:17–21). Now in this center portion of the Gospel we find three more stories,[1] connected with each other, but also connected with the above-mentioned stories. Is there any thread, other than bread itself, that unites all of these stories? When we look at them together our initial response is to notice that conflict is present in them all. In the opening segment we saw how the stories reveal plotting, intrigue, and suspicion on the part of the Pharisees, etc. It reveals a struggle about authority, power, status and position. In the last section of the Gospel it will initiate, and be at the center of, the conflict that culminates in the crucifixion of Jesus. In this present section conflict overshadows the apparent quiet. It rings out in the command and warning of Jesus, "Beware of the leaven of the Pharisees and the leaven of Herod."

Not only is conflict present in all three sections but there is a sense in which it spreads. Initially, in the opening chapters of the Gospel, the conflict involves the Pharisees over against Jesus and the disciples. In this middle section it involves the disciples over against Jesus. In the final section it seems to involve Jesus himself in his absence/presence, life/death, in the abandonment sequence of which we will say more later. The conflict will have spread then from the outside to the inside. In that last sequence it seems that the whole meal is clearly placed in direct relationship to, both as balance and counterpoint, the passion events themselves, as Jesus enters into his death. There appears then to be some connection between the presence of bread and the presence of conflict.

This association of bread with conflict is not something new to Mark. It has a previous history in the Scripture. In Genesis we read the story of Melchizedek, king of Salem, king of peace. Bread is a food that he and Abraham share, but they share it following the conflict that involved the defeat of the kings (Gen 14:18). Similarly we find in the story of the exodus the event concerning the manna that

God gave his people as he led them out of the conflict and bondage of the Egyptians. The psalmist commenting on the event says, "He commanded the skies above, and opened the doors of heaven; and he rained down on them manna to eat, and he gave them the grain of heaven; men ate the bread of angels; he sent them food in abundance" (Ps 78:3–5).

It is further worthy of note that in all these stories the land is also involved. In Mark we have pointed already to the land on both sides of the lake. Jesus crosses the water to include the new Gentile land and embrace it and its people in the Kingdom. In the other meal we mentioned above, between Abraham and Melchizedek, we notice that it involves a Jew and a Gentile. The meal is a sign of shared hospitality in this moment. Similarly too it is in the context of God leading his people to a new land, a new truth, a new vision of things, a new relationship with him that he feeds the people at the exodus. Following the proposal of the covenant in Exodus 19:3 the ratification of the event takes place through a meal.[2] Campbell comments, in his work on mythology, on an old custom called land-naming. He comments on how in the act of land-naming people frequently revert to the old places and stories and events that had great significance for them.[3] We see this even in the naming of many towns, cities, and even states in America. This process enables people to connect with their previous experience, and also it brings the very land itself into the dynamism of their lives. It comes then as no surprise that in Mark, as in the exodus when a new land is being explored and claimed, when Jesus is journeying through the new pagan territory and reaching out to embrace the land and the people, the old symbol reappears. As in the journey from Egypt to the promised land "manna" was a powerful symbol and food for the people, so now bread is going to be a focal symbol for Mark in this new journey of Jesus.

Another interesting facet emerges as we gaze even more fully and at greater length on the Markan feeding stories. In the story of the feeding of five thousand on the Jewish side of the lake the apparent problem of the followers' hunger is proposed by the disciples. It is they who come to him. It is they who perceive the loneliness of the place, the hunger of the people, the lateness of the time, and it is they who draw Jesus' attention to this. Mark puts it as follows, "It was getting late. His disciples came to him and said, 'It is already very late; this is a lonely place. Send the people away. Let them go to the nearby farms and villages and buy themselves something to eat'" (6:34). By contrast in the second story (8:1) the feeding of the four thousand, the problem here is perceived by Jesus. It is now he who goes to them. He "called the disciples to him and said 'I feel sorry for these people because they have been with me for three days now and have nothing to eat. If I send them home without feeding them they will faint as they go because some of them have come a long way.'" Here then it is Jesus who is the observant one, who initiates the dialogue, and who moves the perceived problem toward some resolution.

In both of these stories eating is involved under the direction of Jesus. We have traditionally focused on the Eucharist as the paradigm of the meal Jesus shared with people. That however was a special meal, given for a special group in rather special circumstances. He had many other kinds of meals with them and with others such as rogues and sinners and ruffians. These meals had a slightly different flavor. Here Jesus is sharing an ordinary meal and caring for the physical needs of the people. He is offering to them the kind of sustenance they need to live. In fact in the second story this point is emphasized. They will "faint

as they go because some of them have come a long way."
It is then an ordinary meal but nevertheless eating is important. In fact Rahner points out how the process of eating
and nutrition is itself an extraordinary human event. It is by
this means that man takes into himself nutrition which is
then assimilated into "human stuff" which is capable of
becoming conscious and reflecting on itself.⁴ Thus to eat a
meal with someone is to participate in a very sacred event.
It is celebrating the very process of transformation; it is celebrating and participating in death and life.⁵

There is a third bread story in this section which has
great significance and adds to our understanding of the
bread theme. In fact it brings this section to a close. The
event is recorded in 8:13. It begins with the last boat trip,
the sixth and final crossing of the lake. Here too, as on so
many other occasions, a conflict breaks out between Jesus
and the disciples. Jesus makes the observation. "They had
forgotten to bring bread with them and they had but one
loaf with them in the boat." The disciples fail to see the significance of this and so they maintain a debate among
themselves, deploring the lack of loaves.⁶ This now is the
third time that we have bread as the central theme in the
section, and this itself is highly significant. Whenever there
is a threefold repetition, Mark uses it to indicate development of the character until in the final repetition he fully
reveals the meaning.⁷ This is the third emphasis on bread.
Already the conflict has been present in the other two scen-
arios but now it is clear that the drama between Jesus and
the disciples has peaked. They just don't understand at all
about the loaf.

Jesus reacts to this situation by trying to expand their
consciousness through a series of questions. The questions
point on the one hand to the truth of the situation, while
on the other they reflect a kind of sarcasm. The following

questions then emerge in the story, and it is also interesting to observe that in this section there are seven questions:[8] Why are you arguing? Do you not yet perceive or understand? Are your hearts hardened? Having eyes do you not see? Do you not remember a. when I broke the five loaves? b. when I broke the seven loaves? How is it that you do not understand? It is obvious that Jesus is leading their consciousness in a direction and equally obvious that they do not understand what he is trying to help them see. "They are in fact in that danger against which Jesus is warning them and are approaching that condition which normally characterizes the unbelieving outsider: seeing but not perceiving, hearing but not understanding. Their heart is hardened since the great meal; they have understood nothing of Jesus' messianic ministry and also at the walk on the water they did not grasp the mystery of Jesus' person."[9]

In this dialogue Jesus is rather forceful. He comes back to the disciples again and again stressing the abundance he is for them. He does everything he can to try to get them to see. He pushes them even to the awareness of the symbolic numbers in the hope they will see. How many baskets were left? Twelve, they answered. And when I broke the seven loaves for the four thousand how many baskets full of leftover pieces did you take up? Seven, they answered. Notice the numbers twelve, seven, four, seven. All of them are richly symbolic within their tradition. They speak of abundance, fullness, perfection, of rich harvests and plenty. They are numbers that have a long history in their tradition. There were the seven years of fullness followed by seven years of famine; there were seven years of work to win Rachel and seven more to win Lea. There were the twelve tribes of Israel, the four corners of the earth. All of these were important in Jewish numerology.[10] They should then have perceived the fullness, the abundance, but they did not. Since the voice of abundance is not heard, the voice of scarcity and limitation will be, as we shall see in the next section of the Gospel.

The last symbol of this section on bread is the symbol of the loaf. "They had forgotten to bring any bread along, except for one loaf they had none with them in the boat" (8:14). It has been underlying all the discussion so far. It gathers all the other symbols in the section into itself and it conveys its own central significance to them while embracing theirs. It gathers the conflict, new land and hospitality themes as Jesus, in conflict with those who cannot understand, endeavors to give them a new place within him. It incorporates the themes of eating, of invitation, and abundance as he tries to show them his sufficiency for them and tneir freedom to receive from him. In this final symbol Jesus reveals himself. He identifies himself as the loaf. He is the symbolic object. He is the one loaf in the boat with them even though their consciousness cannot perceive it. He is the invitation, abundance, etc. As the one loaf he alone constitutes the bond between Jew and Gentile. His presence then stands in marked contrast to the concern of the apostles because they have no bread.

This offering of himself as the one loaf is precisely what makes for the crisis here.[11] Will they perceive the central nature and importance of his presence? The disciples, initially the privileged ones, are now clearly joining those who miss the message. Throughout this section Mark has accused them of being, and shown them to be, hard of heart, myopic in perception, filled with ignorance, and lacking in trust and faith. They who initially were called, as we saw, to be bearers of the message, the manifestation of teaching, the agents of Jesus in the ministry, have now become barriers to the growth of the Kingdom. It becomes increasingly clear that if they are going to be truly disciples they must expand their vision and see the whole loaf. Kelber very insightfully makes the following comment: "In 4:11–12 Jesus had separated the twelve and those about him from outsiders and characterized the latter as people who look and look, but do not see, who hear and hear, but do not understand. By applying this outside characterization to the disciples Mark has in fact cast them to the outside. While the charge hardness of heart put the disciples into the role of opposition, that of blindness and deafness reveals that they are about to forfeit their privileged position as insiders. The followers are on the way of becoming opponents and the insiders outsiders."[12]

In terms of a story of the self what seems to be happening here is an endeavor to break through to a new vision, a new balance. The "who I am" question is opened again. Sometimes this comes about from the self who notices the hunger and poverty of the personality. Sometimes it comes about through the consciousness that I have of myself (ego) as being insufficient. I reach for a deeper self to nurture and feed my life. It seems then that a new answer must be given to the "messianic secret," to the question that lies at the center of my own existence. There is a clash emerging at a deeper level than previously experienced. With the development of the person the ego emerges out of the unconscious. The conscious mind, the operating ego is then likely to presume that it is the answer to the "who I am" question. Such a statement however reflects only its own fragility because then it defines itself only with reference to the past. At the same time the deeper self, the Christ image as we call it, keeps pushing its own cause. It refuses to be defined by the past but keeps pushing to the future. It is on the journey toward wholeness, unity, completeness and invites me to identify the loaf. What becomes clear is that I cannot. I want to get to that standpoint and yet I cannot. What is abundantly clear to me now is that I am so sure I know the answer that I have totally lost even the question. Inflation is the glossy side of alienation.

Jesus in the Gospel is pointing to bread as the source of life and to himself as the loaf. By being united in the loaf the two sides of the lake are united. The disciples however are only united in the bread (not unlike the Cana story in John where they are said to see the sign and miss the signification or better still symbolization). They remain at the level of picture thinking, of visual images, without going through the image as mediator, and, as Lonergan says, "visual images are incapable of representing or suggesting the normative exigencies of intelligence and reasonableness and much less their power to effect the intentional self-transcendence of the subject."[13] The key question is: What is the image triggering in me? What reality is it manifesting? To catch that would be to see what it is precisely that the disciples do not see. Failure to see the loaf, and through the loaf, or, as Ricoeur would say, to the world projected by the loaf, is for Mark the great tragedy. But that is where I am. I can believe now that I must come to see through the loaf, that I want to perceive life from the point of view of wholeness, totality, harmony, but the truth is that I cannot see beyond the immediate, beyond the bread. For sight to occur now I first need insight. The symbol of the loaf is particularly apt to bring this segment of the Gospel to a close because it gathers together much of what the trip across the lake was all about. The loaf is at once the bread that nourishes and as such is a feminine symbol. On the other hand it is the fruit of the seed which was plunged into the earth and as such is masculine. It is formed by man and in turn it forms man. It is the stuff of life offered throughout the ages for the benefit of man.

Chapter 11
Blindness and Sight

We turn now to a new moment in the development of our existence and our life. When I say new moment I do not mean to indicate something that has not been progressing all along. I mean that a new phase, or emphasis, begins. This phase opens up now for us the spiritual meaning of our lives. It has been blossoming at its own rate of development all through our growing years as Allport has so carefully documented.[1] Now however the religious question seems to come more and more to the forefront of existence, or at least it seems to want to do so, even though it is frequently blocked. Jung puts it like this: "Among all my patients in the second half of life, that is to say over thirty-five, there has not been one whose problem in the last resort was not that of finding a religious outlook on life."[2] Jung seems to indicate thirty-five as the mid-point in life. Others[3] however have given different figures for either its onslaught or its completion, but nearly all psychologists, poets, and literary people testify to this strange phenomenon called mid-life.

103

In Mark's Gospel Scripture scholars extend the mid-section from Chapter 8 to 11 approximately. It exists within two stories having to do with blind men. Within these two stories Mark works out the meaning of the section as a whole. We will deal with these two stories here and then proceed to consider the rest of the section in the following chapters. The two stories make it clear that blindess is one of the key symbols of this section. In itself this is a paradox, because the stories indicate that one must first see the blindness, and then the blindess will enable us to see. The stories summon me to identify the blindness within me. As that begins to happen it becomes equally evident that I cannot do that at all. I cannot even name the blindness. This then shows me what really controls my life. What I hope to do in this chapter is to look at the two stories that form the frame for the picture that exists between them. We will look at them as individual stories and then in relation to each other. This will enable us to see a growth in the section as a whole. Then we can look at the key symbol in both stories and in the light of that see the picture or question they hold in tension.

In the first story (8:22), Jesus is at Bethsaida when a blind man is brought to him by some friends. Jesus first places spittle on the man's eyes. Then in an unusual gesture he touches the man's eyes a second time. The man's blindness is cured and Jesus instructs him to go home. There are a number of interesting factors that stand out. The healing here is not instantaneous, the only time when this is not so in the Gospel. It involves a number of touches. Sight only comes gradually. As the sight returns subjects are reduced to objects, and people look like trees. One is left wondering if this is not the real blindness. The man himself is left nameless. He does not reveal himself, which is important, since naming something is equivalent to having control over it. Who or what controls or owns this man's life? In the end Jesus leads him out of the village, which is a very significant action. Villages are small places. They promote intimacy, community and friendship. They make a certain way of life easily accessible and acceptable. But they are also the problem spots for many people. Everyone knows everybody's business. It's easy to get trapped into stereotypical patterns of perception, thought and behavior. Gossip is rampant. They can be very cruel places. They can then be real parochial enclaves in the worst sense of the word. People in villages tend to look backward, to allow themselves to be defined solely in terms of their past and to be limited by it. Jesus, it seems, leads the man out of the stultifying existence and opens for him a larger horizon.

Before proceeding to the second story, what we have already seen seems to have some implications for us in terms of a story of the self. The gradual healing helps me to realize that health usually comes slowly. Man needs his slow unfolding. Most of us need our defenses.[4] They play an important part in protecting us from threats to our self-esteem and security. We will alter them only gradually and generally with a lot of non-threatening encouragement. Levinson calls the task of midlife "the task of disillusionment . . . a reduction of the illusions, a recognition that long held assumptions and beliefs about self and world are not true. . . . It is to become cynical, estranged, unable to believe in anything."[5] What helps with the process of disillusionment is the gradual lessening of defenses, the identification of the current strategies of defense and the relinquishing or altering of them to less extreme measures. In his book *Stories to the Dark* William O'Brien makes the following observation about Dante in his journey in the *Divine Comedy:* frequently "the journey into the dark is never taken because of the preoccupations crowding into the life on the one

hand and the inclination to be fascinated with one's own
fancies of the other. . . . Virgil takes Dante not away from
hell's emissary but right into its jaws."[6] And he describes
this as a "journey in which Dante is willing to let go of the
images that define the life, images that hold us like a vessel,
and accepting in their place images that free the soul on the
journey to God."[7]

The second story of the blind man, given in 10:46, portrays a different vision for us. In this second story the man
is named. He is called Bartimaeus. This blind man is alone
apparently. He is sitting by the side of the road and he hears
Jesus passing along the road. He makes some inquiries and
then calls out to Jesus to help him. Jesus heals him and the
man jumps up and follows Jesus up the road. This man contrasts sharply with the one in the first story. The story
begins with the rather innocent looking statement "as he
was leaving Jericho." This however is not some little unim-
portant, hardly recognizable village. This is a place of considerable importance in the history of the people. It was
from Jericho that Joshua began the conquest of the promised land.[8] George Montague points out that it was "some
eighteen miles from Jerusalem, a resting place for pilgrims
before the last portion of their journey." This man is on the
road to freedom, the beginning of the ultimate journey.
Mark gives this man a name. He is called Bartimaeus. This
man has named his fear as his very name indicates. He has
identified the fear within himself and therefore is in a much
stronger position than the previous man. He knows what
he needs and Mark portrays him as one not easily side-
tracked. He knows where he is and he puts himself in Jesus'
way. He is not quiet, passive, or silent. He is determined,
vociferous and assertive. He is not concerned with the need
of approval from the crowd or moved by the need of self-
esteem. He is aware of his need for healing and he goes in

search of it. He addresses Jesus in a very unusual way for any of the Markan characters: "Jesus, son of David, have mercy on me."

Jesus invites the blind man to come closer, and when the man approaches he challenges him to state what it is he is looking for from him. The blind man by his answer indicates that he (blind man) is not the ultimate answer to his own destiny. There is then in the story a tension between his assertiveness and independence on the one hand and his powerlessness and dependence on the other. There is both structure and spontaneity in the blind man's life. On the one hand he sits by the side of the road; on the other hand he knows what is going on. He is at the side of the road, the observer position; nevertheless, he finds his way to the center of action. He is sitting, a position of dependence; nevertheless "he casts off the mantle" and "begins to follow Jesus up the road." Henceforth whatever it is that is at the "end of the road" is the new horizon for his life.

The first story is linked with Caesarea, the place of departure. The second story is linked with Jerusalem, the place of arrival for Jesus and the disciples. Between these two stories, the departure and the arrival, are a series of sayings which are called "way sayings." They are comments that Jesus makes as he moves along, but like the boat trip in the previous section these sayings provide a unifying theme in this section. There are six such sayings, and they can be viewed as either a series of questions or as a core question. I have chosen to deal with it as a core question and will focus on it in the next chapter. Around these sayings are the two stories of the blind men. They act as a frame for the picture which the sayings are. The two go together, one enlightening the other, but now we turn our attention to the blind men and the blindness.

What then of the central symbol of blindness itself? What is it pointing toward in my life? If I could begin to catch that, then perhaps I could begin to start to see. Michael Crosby[9] speaks of certain "attitudes or looks that keep us from inner commitment." Borrowing from Richard Byrne's work[10] he lists different kinds of look which he sees as obstacles. These would be similar to the kinds of look that would point toward what I think the blindness in my life might be. I will list Crosby's looks here and then add two of my own categories:

1. The first look he describes as the curious look, or an attitude of being full of cares and anxieties. People who are rooted in curiosity he describes as "reflecting a kind of chaos, a separation, an alienation within themselves. . . . They are outside themselves figuratively and literally." The person whose curiosity is in charge of his life is like a fly who is moving everywhere, never still anywhere, constantly in motion, constantly going from one thing to another. This means that we are controlled as Crosby says by "those who tell us what we need to be accepted," the advertisers, etc. We delegate control of our life then, and of our vision about life's meaning, purpose, etc. to others, expecially to those who control the media.

2. The lustful look which "seeks pleasure," "instant gratification" and "instant relief." The lustful look seeks the immediate. It cannot wait, delay or postpone. There is an element of necessity to it. I must have this and I must have it now. And if I do not get it there is a resulting depression. He suggests that if we look at our depressions and see how we respond to them we will discover how the lustful look controls our lives and what the specific object of our lust and pleasure is now in vogue.

3. The third look that leads to what I have called blindness, or that reflects it, is what Crosby calls the "ideal look." This shows us the eyes of comparison. We are forever wondering how we are doing as opposed to how someone else is doing. This comparison takes the form of "more or less" and "better or worse." Our view of our life and our self then becomes measured against the attainment of our idealized image. Karen Horney shows how the "idealized image precisely to the extent that it is unrealistic tends to make a person arrogant."[11] Three possibilities occur when the idealized look or image is in control according to Horney. Either (1) the person thinks he is his idealized image, which leaves him with a God complex, or (2) he is not his idealized image, in which case he is by comparison highly despicable, or (3) he is aware of the gap between the idealized image and the reality, in which case he is always compulsive, trying to bridge the gap and whip himself into perfection. We end up then frustrated, arrogant, angry and judgmental.

4. The final look that Crosby lists is the resentful look which he also calls the look of unforgiveness. This is the look that holds on to anger, holds on to hurt and pain and thrashes around in it. We are then dominated and controlled by the anger and the interior feelings. Resentment and anger that is cultivated within is the most insidious of all emotions and it acts toward destruction. It has in terms of relationships many different disguises inclusive of withdrawal, silence, headaches, backaches, ridicule, constant agreeing or disagreeing, etc., and in ninety-five percent of all such people there is a constant avoidance of eye contact. These are truly eyes that do not see.

5. Vacant look. I have chosen to add two other categories to those listed by Crosby. The vacant look is reflected in the eyes that are attentive to other times, places or events. In the midst of a conversation, sometimes even as a way of existence, a person will trigger out. He will go on a vacation and a vacant non-seeing look will come over the eyes. This is the look of the lost. They expect nothing from anyone, they expect nothing from themselves, and generally they don't end up disappointed.

6. The onlooker. This too is a look that leads to blindness. It stands outside and away from events and people. Distancing is its viewing tool. To look in this manner is to look while trying to avoid contact. It needs the constancy of separation lest it be overwhelmed. The danger however is that it only sees what it wants to see. It only sees with physical eyes and not with the deeper eyes of the person. It loses one and blinds him to his own assumptions, expectations and limitations.

Crosby finds that the way out of this blindness, out of these obstacles to vision, is by entering the "circle of care." We need, he says, to be "grounded in authentic cares." There is in the Markan story another symbol in this midsection that leads our thoughts in a similar direction. The "child" is placed by Jesus in the middle of the disciples (9:35–38). This action by Jesus effectively raises the question of the disciples' attitude in regard to the child. Their attitude is reflected in the incidents that follow. They attempt to prevent the children getting to Jesus but Jesus will rebuke them for this attitude.

The child then is an important question in this midsection. What is the blindness pointing toward in me and what is the child pointing toward? Jesus, the self center, places the child before me and asks: What is your attitude toward the child? Jung notes that "one of the essential pictures of the child motif is futurity. The child is potential future ... even though at first sight it might seem like a retrospective configuration. Life is a flow, a flowing into the future, and not a stoppage on a backwash. .... In the individuation process it anticipates the figure that comes from the synthesis of conscious and unconscious elements in the personality. It is therefore a unifying symbol which unites the opposites, a mediator, bringer of healing, that is, one who makes whole."[12] Erikson too places great emphasis on the mid-life crisis and sees it as a time that we must face the child question, only for him that means looking to the next generation. It is a time when man looks over his life to see what he has generated or helped to generate and begins to face old age with a sense of integrity or despair.[13]

The child then stands as an important symbol in the midst of the blindness and darkness. I look at the child both within and without. I wonder what I have helped to generate in life. I wonder what I want to bring to birth now. The child puts me in touch with all that is young and growing, alive and full of possibilities, that is hope for the future, that is the promise of possibility in me. It also puts me in touch with vulnerability, fragility and dependency. Jesus confronting the apostles is raising with them and for them the transition between young and old and invites them to seek new ways of being young/old.[14] The two symbols, the child and the blindness, point to something within. The blindness must be perceived, the child must be nourished and nurtured and believed, before the whole person can dance and jump and follow the self up the road.

Chapter 12
The Returning Question

In the last chapter I pointed out how there is a question concerning suffering and death that keeps coming back between 8:22 and 10:52. This question arises in three different places (8:31; 9:30; 10:31). Not only that, but it appears to be more than a haphazard thing. The question is directed to an ever growing group of people, with an ever increasing intensity and clarity, and it emerges from a consistent center. We will comment briefly on each occurrence:

1. The first mention of it comes at Caesarea Philippi. "And he began to teach them that the Son of Man must suffer many things, be rejected by the elders, chief priests and scribes, be put to death, and after three days rise again." This particular passage occurs at Caesarea Phillippi at the beginning of the journey. It is given against a particular background of expectation. The people are expecting a particular kind of Messiah, and the reference to Isaiah's suffering servant poem doesn't gain much of a hearing. In this particular passage the reference is rather veiled.

The message is not exactly clear, and it is given to a rather general audience.

2. In 9:30 the message comes as they are on the way through Galilee. Here the audience is also more focused. It is directed to the disciples. The announcement itself is also more to the point. It is short and pointed. He says to them, "The Son of Man is to be betrayed into the hands of men. They will kill him and, having been killed, he will rise again on the third day."

3. The third announcement of the question comes in 10:31 as they are on the way to Jerusalem. It's as if the question is there at all three points, the beginning, the middle, and the end. It signals the onset of the midsection of the Gospel, it is the dominant note of it, and it returns at the end of it in full force. This time, Mark notes, he "drew the twelve aside and spoke of things that were going to happen to him" (v. 32). The group here are more intimate than the others, and furthermore the message now is itself unmistakable, Jesus is insistent. He wants the message and the question inherent in it to reach their hearts and minds. The leaders must be willing to accept suffering and death within their concept of Messiah. There is also now more detail about the manner and place of death. "They were now on the way, going up to Jerusalem. Jesus was walking in front of them. They were in dismay. Those who followed were afraid. Once again Jesus took the twelve aside and spoke of the things that were going to happen to him. 'Listen,' he told them, 'we are going up to Jerusalem where the Son of Man will be handed over to the chief priests and teachers of the law. They will condemn him to death and then hand him over to the Gentiles. These will make fun of him, spit on him,

whip him, and kill him. And after three days he will rise
to life.'"

The returning question then is being issued in three different locations geographically; it becomes clearer with
each new announcement, and it becomes more focused in
terms of those to whom it is addressed.

It is also interesting to note that the reaction of the
apostles on all three occasions is oppositional. In the first
incident Jesus rebukes Peter. Then Peter rebukes Jesus. The
"rebuke" is a technical term in Mark's Gospel. It is indicative of exorcism language.[1] Peter is strongly opposing what
Jesus has just announced. In the second incident things get
a little worse. The apostles not only don't understand what
Jesus is saying but now they are "afraid to ask." When Jesus
on the third occasion introduces the same topic, we note
that they are now "filled with alarm, and the people who
followed behind were afraid." There is then an inverse progression. The question and Jesus are moving with insistency
to greater clarity. The apostles on the other hand are
becoming more frightened and now even afraid of allowing
their thoughts and feelings to enter into consciousness.
They try to repress the emerging insight. Hence of course
the blindness.

Theodore Weeden[2] in his study of Mark's Gospel sees
a progressive deterioration in the disciples' relationship to
Jesus not just in the above passages but indeed throughout
the whole Gospel. He maintains that the disciples as presented in Chapters 1–8 are unable to perceive who Jesus is
despite the manner in which he constantly heals, exorcises,
etc., the people who come to him. This "non-perceptive-
ness" grows "into" or rather deteriorates to a "misconception" of who Jesus is in the midsection of the Gospel, which
embraces the three passages we are considering. Finally a

third phase is reached which he calls a stage of "rejection" which is inaugurated with Judas' decision to betray Jesus to the hierarchy in 14:10. For Weeden "Christology is the issue that divides Jesus and his confidants."[3] He sees Mark as emphasizing the fact that authentic messiahship is indeed suffering messiahship and he maintains that Mark underscores this (a) through the suffering role of Jesus in the passion predictions, (b) through the motif of the disciples' misconception of messiahship, (c) by devoting extensive attention to its corollary suffering discipleship, and (d) by giving central importance to the passion narrative.[4] While one may find some disagreement with Weeden's desire to paint the disciples as the opponents of Jesus, one can hardly argue with the general tonality of his observations. The disciples are blind, and the symbolism in the Gospel is very clear on that point. No one comes to see what kind of Messiah Jesus is, and that is particularly marked in the three passages that I have phrased the "returning question."

What is it then that the disciples cannot see but that they must see and accept if they are to make progress? What is the returning question? Is it not clearly the question of suffering and death? The disciples need to hear this but cannot. Their attention is focused elsewhere. They cannot, or at least do not, hear what Christ is saying to them. His attempt to raise the issue meets with their attempt to deny it. Where then is the disciples' attention riveted? The other incidents in Chapters 8–11 provide the answer. We will list a few:

1. They are concerned, on the conscious level, with questions of personal status, power and ambition. Jesus has to confront them on this at Capernaum. "What," he asks, "were you arguing about on the road?" He represents a

compensatory attitude. He calls them not to power but to death, and ultimately to union with God.

2. They are concerned, on the conscious level, with their own inadequacy and failure to cast out an evil spirit from an epileptic boy. He again offers a compensatory point of view, inviting them to trust not in their own limited capacities but in the presence of God among them.

3. They are concerned, on the conscious level, with their own comfort and therefore don't want people bringing children around. Again he offers a compensatory view and places the "other" in their midst. Their own self-absorption is immediately apparent.

4. They are concerned, on the conscious level, with maintaining their privileged consciousness as evident in the transfiguration scene. They want to stay put and build three booths there. Again Jesus compensates for their limited knowledge by inviting them to an exchange of life, in short, to death.

5. The symbols and stories in this mid-section multiply the distractions, etc., that the apostles use to keep away the returning question. We will comment briefly on the story of the rich man in 10:17 as illustrative of this point. This young man is somewhat discontented. He has a sense of wasting his life away. He is in what Jung might call the "I'm stuck" phase of life. He is extremely manipulative and so addresses Jesus with the greeting "Good Teacher." Jesus however reads the set-up and refuses to play the game. "Why do you call me good?" he asks, thereby absenting himself from having to conform to the other's greeting. Not only is the man manipulative, he is

also impetuous. He is impatient and in a hurry. He runs to Jesus, he kneels before him, and he addresses him. He is also very function-oriented. Accomplishments are important to him and he is able to give his credentials. He also asks the functioning question, "What must I do?"

This man however is also more deeply rooted than it might first appear. He is in search of an ultimate meaning to his life. He is already a "good man." He has accomplished a lot, as he tells us: "Ever since I was young I have obeyed all the commandments." Three times in the story we are told that Jesus looked at him or the disciples. This look is in contrast with the looks we mentioned in the last chapter. This is the look of love. It is an inviting look. He asks him into a deeper relationship. It invites him to (a) go and sell, (b) give to the poor, and (c) come and follow. The rich man cannot do this and that is tragic. What is the obstacle? This time it is wealth.

Jesus points out to the disciples how wealth is the obstacle. How difficult it is for the rich man, he says, and he repeats it. The disciples are shocked because it clearly clashes with their expectations. In their tradition wealth is a sign of God's favor. Here it is an obstacle. Harrington comments, "If he begins by stressing the difficulty of access to the Kingdom for the wealthy he quickly passes to the difficulty of entering the Kingdom at all. The repeated 'how hard' ... to enter the Kingdom of God frames the amazement of the disciples. That amazement grows to astonishment when they realize that the warning has been aimed at them."[5] Why is wealth such an obstacle? Because we are so prone to see in it our status, power, security, happiness, and indeed, even at times, our identity. The call of Jesus however is to a deeper relationship. It is a call to trust God and to take him seriously. The effect of the message is immediate: "And they were

exceedingly astonished and asked: Who then can be
saved? Jesus looked at them and said, 'With men it is
impossible, but not with God, for all things are possible
with God'" (v. 26–27).

Told as a story of the self the message of the mid-section of the Gospel opens us at the midpoint of life to the
question of reversals and of death. It is that time in life
when we are frequently losing children to their own way of
life, and parents to the finality of death. In between the
question of our own death surfaces. It is precisely here, I
believe, that the religious question emerges with force. It
has been present all along but now it strikes home like
never before. We become like the rich young man in search
of an ultimate meaning. The question returns again and
again. Ernest Becker, commenting on both Rank and Kier-
kegaard, says, "Both men reached the same conclusion after
the most exhaustive psychological quest: that at the farthest
reaches of scientific description psychology has to give way
to theology, that is, to a world view that absolves the individual's conflict and guilt and offers him the possibility of
some kind of heroic apotheosis."[6] Man comes to contact the
meaning of his life in confrontation with the meaning of his
death. The two are not separable.

Looking backward over my own poetry I see the elements of this question pressing in upon my consciousness
from the self.[7] I expressed it first like this:

O cursed respectability
Thou insane sanity,
Thou ever active sin in me,
You hold me back from madness,
From life and love, in the
Cross' fierce intensity.

The "respectability" of that poem is the obstacle that needed to be broken as I was beginning to realize in a passage from a later poem:

> Entry to the kingdom
> By way of the void
> Demands that men be broken
> The agony and crucifixion
> Both have spoken.

In a still later poem it returns again in a stroll I took along Jones Beach in April:

> I stood today
> At the seasons' critical point
> That in between moment of
> Winter and spring.
> Touched was I again by the
> Futility of life, evident in
> Limpid limbs of former energy
> Now atrophied, and eyes
> Glazed nostalgically, lost
> On the sea's glassy face, reflecting sun;
> Bundled in scarves of colorless similarity
> Behind which sunken cheeks and unshaven jaws
> Testified to life's lost fullness.

The question keeps returning. The self keeps insisting that a major crack must occur. Perhaps this is why James Zullo can define this stage of life as a "crisis of limits." The limits come crashing into our awareness in simple events as well as in more traumatic ones. I begin to notice my hair thinning out; my powers of concentration dwindle; my body doesn't seem to be able to do as much as once it did. Sometimes, as the Gospel stories in this section indicate, more traumatic events occur. I face again my life's commitment. I am married but I wonder how well. I am ordained but how committed am I? I have labored in life but for what? Life seems to start collapsing and sometimes anxiety and depression find their way to the surface. Our fears begin to surface and sometimes we identify with them, thus blocking out any progress. We become bullies of children, or sometimes our power drive re-emerges and we search for the best places at table like James and John, or we try to become so self-righteous that we have no more time for other demons and resent those who cure in the name of Jesus.

In this moment questions keep coming. Nothing really ever totally blocks them out. Gradually the questions begin to assume a face. I find myself wondering if I am ultimately alone before an uncaring, unconcerned and indifferent universe. I look around at my achievements and accomplishments. I notice my friends and my values. Even as all of this is happening I hear again and again the question of life and death, of what lasts and what fades, of what matters and what is peripheral, and I begin to realize, at first perhaps in a vague way, my need to be connected to an ultimate. I realize in a dim sort of way that I am alone and that no friends, no ritual, no routine, nothing will save me from the question that keeps coming into my life. Death becomes my question in the midst of living. Teilhard speaks of the need for a radical excentration, a return to God that can only be accomplished by dying, and as I listen I realize more and more that this is true.[8]

The returning question leads us through its own journey with its own stages, outlines and contours. Kübler-Ross has documented and given structure to the process of death and dying.[9] She speaks of the psychological crisis undergone by the "patient." Peter Kreeft attempts to study death from a more philosophical point of view, and in the working out of his theory he suggests five faces that we encounter successively.[10] Mayer suggests that there are three moments or phases in the rite of passage as she attempts a descriptive analysis of the mid-life situation.[11] All of them, however, speak of it as a crisis, a new experience of the nothingness we spoke of earlier, a new meeting with the void or whatever inhabits it. This is the new sense of reality that the self invites us to enter in mid-life. We are called to disillusionment, to "recognize the emptiness, terror, and formlessness at the center of human consciousness," and that we "only glimpse the emptiness, terror and formlessness by virtue of our honesty and courage."[12]

What the self is doing then is stripping away the illusions. What is coming is irreversible whether we accept it or not. The Peter in me may not want to accept the inevitability of death but it is coming anyway. We begin to see that sometimes even against our will "persons, things, experiences, relationships, civilizations, all the things borne upon us by the river of time, are borne away, a world sliding down and away every second into the darkness never to return."[13] The self summons us into an uncertain future. It calls us to follow, to face its reality, to abandon our illusions, to accept our mortality, to live from meaning and for meaning, to become one who will follow its leadership "up the road."

Chapter 13
The Transfiguration

There are many different attempts made by Scripture scholars to locate, explain, understand and interpret the story of the transfiguration. Some see it as a story that belongs to the ressurection period;[1] others completely disagree.[2] Rosemary Haughton reduces the discussion with the simple observation that the story is "poetry and theology and that it is simplest to suppose that the writers were doing what they said they were doing . . . giving us as clear an account as possible of something that happened in the sight of three men who afterward recounted their experience to others as well as they could."[3] In the midst of these discussions Kelber with his usual precision makes the interesting observation that Mark certainly places the story in the middle of the Gospel. It forms, he says, "the central scene of the whole Gospel story. It constitutes the high mountain scene in Mark's Gospel."[4] For Haughton also, even though her observations are based on the Lukan account, the fact that the story occupies the center position in the Gospel is highly significant. She says that for her it is between the foreshadowing and the fulfillment; it is neither one nor the other, but it is also in the middle in that it takes place "across the boundaries, releasing one (sphere) into another in the oddest way."[5] In the Markan story it is not only in the middle of the Gospel but it is also carefully placed against the backdrop of the "passion predictions" and the "on the way" sayings we referred to previously.

There are a number of elements in the story that are worth commenting on before we try to see the significance of the story as a whole for the self. Mark introduces the story by saying, "Six days later." This is rather unusual, for Mark, as a general rule, is not given to providing us with such exact information. It is interesting to note that Luke, whose Gospel has a great deal of temple language, liturgical language, says that the event took place eight days later. Luke's and Mark's selection of the time frame would then appear to be purposive. The six days are meant to indicate something. In our attempt to understand it, we can notice that it is not the only place in Scripture where "six days" are mentioned. There are for instance, the six days of creation in the Book of Genesis, after which, we are told, God rested. In the Book of Exodus we are told of the six days customarily set aside as a period of preparation before an encounter with God. Moses after six days of preparation hears the voice of God, and God's glory is revealed. John in the opening of his Gospel gives us the six days of the new creation before the culminating event of the marriage feast of Cana on the seventh day. The inclusion then of this remark by Mark seems to have symbolic value. It points to a period of preparation that is coming to an end. Something new is about to happen. It has about it the feel of creation or beginning. This first understanding is enriched when we look at the next two little details that Mark uses in his story.

Mark says that Jesus took Peter, James, and John "apart" and led them to a "high mountain." Both the idea of being taken apart and the idea of the mountain seem to go together frequently in Scripture. Throughout the Scriptures people are called apart from the community as a sign of specialness, or for a special purpose or reason. Jesus himself is frequently seen to go apart from the disciples. John Sheets in fact points to a pattern that this constitutes for Jesus in Scripture. He says that in Mark Jesus goes apart or "prays at key moments in his public life . . . which has to do with establishing the Kingdom," and he contrasts this with the Lukan Gospel where prayer, he suggests, is the characteristic atmosphere of Christ's life.[6] This then reinforces the idea of special election. Again the fact that not all the apostles are witnesses to this moment is important. It is only the three, Peter, James and John, who are present. On each of the four occasions in the Gospel when they are with Jesus on their own it seems that something unusual, in fact something revelatory, occurs. In 5:36 it is their witnessing the raising of Jairus' daughter, in this chapter it is their witnessing the transfiguration, in 13:3 it is their being told about the end of an era and the beginning of another, and in 14:33 it is the situation of being invited to be present as Jesus prays in Gethsemani. Haughton pays special attention to the selection of these men. Their selection indicates for her that Jesus did not want to be alone at this time when he was wrestling with his own meaning. They were his friends and so he could allow them to see his vulnerability. They were entering into a new "sphere" in their relationships with him, and she suggests that the "door between the worlds, opened with pain and glory, can never be closed again, that there is traffic through it however modest and unnoticeable."[7]

The concept of the mountain intensifies the idea of specialness and uniqueness contained germinally in "being called apart." The two concepts, when placed together, invoke the exodus experience. There the interesting fact is that Moses and the people are called out to be with God. They come to the mountain but it is clear that it is not so much to the mountain as to himself that God has led the people. Notice in Exodus 19:3–9 how frequently the words "me" and "mine," "my people" and "myself" are spoken by Yahweh. God calls Israel to the covenant with him and to the experience of him. The mountain is symbolic of that fact. The whole experience of Israel at Sinai is couched in liturgical language and symbolism. James Plastaras has well attested to this in his work *The God of Exodus*, and he further comments in the light of it that in the Markan story the transfiguration is presented as a new experience of God showing himself to his people. The transfiguration recalls that whole exodus experience in which God speaks through Moses to his people.[8]

In the New Testament we also meet the mountain on several occasions, and on all of these occasions Christ shows himself to the apostles in a special way. There is the mountain of temptation[9] where the trials of the temptation culminate in a new temple in which God is worshiped, the mountain of blessing[10] where the law bursts forth to become grace and truth for all mankind, the mountain of multiplication[11] where the true manna is present for the nourishment of the people, the mountain of agony[12] where the intercession of the new Moses is victorious over the abandonment of God's people, the mountain of Calvary[13] where the new covenant is sealed in the blood of the lamb, the mountain of the ascension[14] where free men are drawn into the intimacy of the Father, and finally the mountain of transfiguration[15] that we are reflecting on here where the love of God shines forth in dazzling brilliance. The mountain thus adds a dimension of revelation, intimacy and teaching to the idea of specialness.

On the mountain two figures appear. These point again in the direction of the importance of this story. Traditionally they are the two important figures of the Old Testament that represent the law and the prophets. They point in the direction of the end time since it was widely believed that "prominent figures of Old Testament history would appear at the end of this world and play a part in the events leading up to it."[16] God then is bringing the whole meaning of the Old Testament to fulfillment. This is the end time now being ushered in. Harrington points out that in Mark the normal order of Moses and Elijah is reversed and sees in the placing of Elijah's name first the fact that the tradition of Elijah being rapt to heaven as the better known tradition."[17] Furthermore he draws our attention to the difference between Luke's and Mark's story. In Luke "Jesus holds center stage. . . . (The disciples) do not share in the revelation but as witnesses of his anticipated glory they will be stronger to support the humiliation of the cross."[18] In Mark, he points out, "Jesus leads the three disciples up a high mountain where he was transfigured before "them." Moses and Elijah appeared "to them," and it was for the disciples' benefit that "a heavenly voice was heard, speaking of Jesus in the third person."[19] Clearly then this experience was for the benefit of the disciples.

In terms of a story of the self, what, if anything, is the significance of this story? William Kraft catches something of what I feel about it when he says in a different context that "a person in his thirties comes to a deeper experience of the holy. In his crisis of nothingness a person's doubts of his religion and of God are critical yearnings for the holy. And concurrently he may feel depressed because he feels that he is losing the ground of his existence. His nothingness, however, is an acute indication of the need for holy ground and a sign of his desperate search for ultimate meaning. . . . He experiences more pressure than in the past to face his need for the holy sense, and his development and involvement in the world give him a greater need for holy transcendence. . . . A person who escapes his nothingness escapes from himself and the holy ground of his life; he is left with a rootless and meaningless life."[20] This sounds very like the experience that occurs in facing the returning question. The bottom seems to drop out of life. Moments of depression begin to invade the person and a new dialogue between the self and the ego ensues. The story asks me to identify the Peter, James and John in me that are being invited to a deeper awareness of the identity of the self, the Jesus center. There is in this new moment a need to be apart, a need to stand open for a new revelation. All of life up to now has only been a preparation. There is forming a new consciousness in the sense that Haughton speaks about when she talks of the exchange of spheres. This is a moment of deep transition, and frequently it is a period of great pain, hurt and confusion. Then with the coming of the vision, there is the desire to remain in the safe place again.

It seems to me that the story of the transfiguration is the same as the story of the returning question, only now it is told from the other side. In the sequence that involved the returning question Jesus was emphasizing the darkness; the self was pressing home the inevitable question. Here the emphasis is on the light side, the new vision of the self. Haughton speaks of the transfiguration story as an "acted out dialectic of a truth so shattering to the normal capacity of the human imagination as to force the barriers of every dayness entirely."[21] Jesus, in other words, broke through to another sphere, not only for himself but also for the apostles. Is there any moment like that in us, or, to put it another way, what does it correspond to in us?

John of the Cross[22] speaks of a moment in the life of a Christian man of prayer which is very similar to what we have in the story. There comes a time, he says, for one who has been following Jesus when he must enter into an altogether new kind of discipleship or sphere. Up to now the disciple has disciplined his life to prayer. He has been faithful to that over a period of time. Initially the disciple has encountered Jesus in what John calls twilight, a time when he is denuded of his need for secure gratification. During this time he will be attracted by Jesus so that he will be strengthened to do battle with his senses and their driving demand to be satisfied. This new moment John calls midnight. What is characteristic here for John is that the person who has gotten this far will often want to turn away from the new sphere to which he is invited and return to the old and more gratifying moment. The new way, or sphere, is difficult. The new stage John describes as being dark and dry to the senses, and it produces in the senses an "inclination to remain alone and in quietude, and the soul will be unable to dwell upon any particular thought, nor will it have a desire to do so."[23]

The transfiguration story seen as a story of the self is pointing in this direction. Something is happening and I don't quite know what it is. There is in my life the consistency of the returning question, the loss of parents who are older, the moving out of the house of my children, the dying of ambition, the re-evaluation of my dreams, the lessening of physical capacities. All of this is going on and yet something else is also happening. A new sphere seems to be opening. I am being brought to quiet, to a deeper and more interior experience. It is an experience that comes at the end of six days, for all of life has been a preparation for it. It's a mountain experience that is revelatory and personalizing. It's a being "called" experience, for it brings with it an awareness of my uniqueness. It is an experience that involves a breakthrough to a new sphere. The powers (Peter, James, John) that incarnated me previously are no longer useful here, at least in the same way. All support systems are found lacking and only the center exists, and the question is: Can you trust it? Is it enough? The ego approaches the self and the meeting is dark and light, awesome and fearful, transforming and transfiguring. What is it that the ego begins to see and sense that constitutes the glory of the self? For a brief period there is an awareness, an illumination, a revelation of where my whole life is going, and together with it the realization that the whole thing makes sense. Elizabeth Boyden Howes catches the flavor of the moment when she comments that in prayer there is a moment that transcends both the I that is operating and the situation in which it is operating. It is a yes-saying moment to a direction that is larger than mine, a purpose that is bigger than mine. Such a moment, she says, is a "marvelous preventer of egocentricity."[24]

Chapter 14
The Temple

At the beginning of Chapter 11 in the Gospel Jesus begins to move toward the city of Jerusalem. This city and the events that occur there will occupy Mark's attention for the next few chapters. At the center of the city is the temple. On three successive days Jesus will approach the temple. Each day he gets closer to the center of the temple and finally he overthrows it. We will approach the three days in sequential order.

On the first day Jesus enters Jerusalem. This entry is interesting and carefully orchestrated by Mark. The journey to Jerusalem has marked Jesus' whole life. It was hinted at in the very beginning and has dominated the movement of his life since Chapter 8. The whole Gospel reaches its climax here in Jerusalem. All of the characters find their fulfillment either positively or negatively in this city. Here all the conflicts of the Gospel are resolved and the drama comes to an apparent close.[1] Jerusalem then is vital to the story, and the way Jesus enters this city thus is important. Characteristically Roman heroes returning from their battles entered their cities with great acclaim. One of the greatest honors given them was to return to Rome itself and have the city turned out by the emperor to greet them and hurl honors before them. This would be very present to the mind of Mark and to the people to whom he wrote. It is surprising then to see the kind of entrance procession that greets Jesus. It is a rather solemn and serious procession. It lacks the joy and fanfare that Matthew's account reports. There are no crowds, no cheering thousands, no mobs laying palms at the feet of the conquering hero. There is no applause and no reading of his glorious exploits. In fact Kelber points out that those who do greet his entrance are not even the residents of the city but those who "went before and who followed."[2] This entrance is not an entrance in glory at all. It is the very opposite. It is the entry of humility, of poverty, in fact of apparent failure. Jesus enters Jerusalem on a "donkey." All his life he seemed to have to borrow things. He got a boat from a poor fisherman, loaves of bread from people who had little to eat, a grave to be buried in from someone who admired him, a cross to be crucified on from his judge, and here a donkey to come home upon.[3] The colt had been tethered which is an interesting observation. The animal had been brought under control, the wild instincts disciplined, the raw energy harnessed. Jesus gives the apostles instructions, orders where the supper will be, indicates how it is to be prepared for and what is to be accomplished, and then he moves to the temple. There is a deliberateness about the move, coming as it does in the late evening.

Not only is Jerusalem the original center of praise and worship but it functions also as a mother image throughout the Old Testament. It is the womb to which the tribes of Israel constantly return. It forms the centerpiece of both their thought pattern and their activity. Joseph Wortman comments on how frequently cities bear feminine names and lists the following examples, "Winnipeg, Roma, Moscow, Babylon, Jerusalem." They are wombs of life. Jesus then in turning to Jerusalem is taking a decisive step. Wortman comments, "His growing awareness of self impels him toward the ultimate symbol of self—maternal Jerusalem."[4] Jesus is moving to a new birthing.

As he moves to Jerusalem he also moves to the center of the city which is the temple. This is the first thing he does when he enters the city. The text does not tell us whether he goes there as a worshiper, a pilgrim, a visitor, an observer, or just because he is curious. It is however a deliberate and strangely mysterious move. Jiminez and O'Connor,[5] commenting on this, draw attention to the paradoxical nature of his relationship to the temple. On the one hand he seems to accept the temple and pay its taxes. On the other hand he rejects what it has become and so chases people out of it. He portrays still a third attitude in indicating a need for its total destruction, and finally a fourth attitude is unveiled when he sees himself as a rival temple to this magnificent symbol that stands at the center of this great city.

This temple, like Jerusalem, has always enjoyed a great reverence among the people. The two go together. Initially in Genesis the temple is the entire universe which by its very existence is caught up in the praise of God. However the "fall" interfered with the fluidity of this praise and introduces a discordant note into its song. The temple then became a man-made building so that man would have in his midst a reminder of the original temple.[6] This new edifice was to serve as a substitute for the world of prayer and praise that was destroyed in the fall. The temple then became a microcosm, a tiny universe in which God's praise could be sung. It was nationalistic in character, a sign of the Jewish world, and this world is about to be destroyed.[7] The old forms of national and egocentric worship must die. A new birth must take place. The destructive pattern of behavior that had become associated with the temple, that had subverted its original and its reconstituted purposes, must pass. Jesus is, as he will claim, the new temple.

This first day corresponds to the beginning of the end. Jesus looks over the temple. He enters it, says nothing and leaves. He has made his appearance in the midst of the chaos and that is sufficient. His very appearance points to a new moment and a new birth. Things can never again be the same. In terms of a story of the self it is the emergence into consciousness of the new center. It is a glimpse of something happening in the midst of the chaos that my old life has become. There is a tiny glimmer that begins; sometimes it is sensed more than seen and from it there is no turning back. Chardin put it like this "Three things, tiny, fugitive; a song, a sunbeam, a glance. . . . So, at first, I thought they had entered into me in order to remain there and be lost in me. On the contrary: they took possession of me and bore me away."[8]

The second visit to the temple occurs on the second day. Here insight gives way to action. The visit is framed by two stories having to do with fig trees. We know by now that this framing technique of Mark is a key to the meaning of the event in the middle. The fig trees are drawing our attention to something. They are important trees in Scripture, providing shade and fruit for the people. They grow in areas that are hard to cultivate and are a sign of the coming of spring and of hope. The destruction of the fig tree is then a key event. When fig trees are fruitless it is catastrophic. Jerusalem is likewise a disaster if she is fruitless. The fig tree and the temple illuminate each other. Jesus relates to both. He curses the one, he replaces the other.

Jesus on this second day enters the temple. Now there is no doubt that he is there as more than a pilgrim, wor-

shiper, or observer. He is there as a man with a mission. He
has come bringing judgment. The temple worship, purpose,
function, position and meaning have all been subverted,
and so it must come to an end. The temple, he says, was no
longer "a house of prayer for all people but a den of
thieves." It is now a place where thieves gather, to bargain,
barter, buy, sell, and change money. Mark draws our attention to the money. It is something that has always fascinated people. Through money people have tried to own,
possess, manipulate, play, be generous, etc. Through
money they have even tried to understand their lives. It
brings with it all kinds of power—freedom to wander, freedom to control, freedom to rebel, freedom to move closer
or away from whatever one desires. It is as Ernest Becker
calls it a powerful "immortality symbol."[9] Money then is
not only a power symbol but also an immortality symbol,
an attempt to create oneself. It means power to "increase
oneself, to change one's natural situation from one of small-
ness, helplessness, finitude, to one of bigness, control, dura-
bility, importance.[10] Casting out the money changers in the
light of this is a very powerful act. Jesus is not only attacking their central religious symbol, he is also attacking their
power system and their method for gaining immortality.

Helen Luke[11] has added to our understanding through
her comments on money. She shows how money originally
came from the goddess in whose temple in Rome the
money was coined. She finds it significant that the money
was coined in the temple of a goddess and not a god. It is
for her a symbolic means of exchange and so belongs to the
feminine principle of relatedness. If the goddess is missing
from the exchange, then what is left is the love of money
itself which is the root of all evil. The coins embodied feeling values, and so when people "earn without paying or

pay without earning, money is divorced from the meaning of exchange."

Entering the temple then on this second day and casting out the money changers, Jesus is bringing to an end a whole way of life that was originally meant to be a canticle of praise. He is pointing toward the destroying power systems, the self-creating immortality systems, and the meaningless exchange systems that have to occupy the zone of the sacred. Listening to the story as a story of the self invites me into my own sources of power, immortality and exchange and forces me to look upon this temple of my own being originally created to be a voice of praise in union with a universe of praise. What is called into question here is my whole life style. The appearance of Jesus on the first day begins the process of insight. His appearance on the second day begins the process of action. The temple must be destroyed, and that begins with the realization that it is a whole life style that is in question. In fact, as the third day shows, it is the meaning of life itself that now begins to emerge as the key question.

Chapter 15
The Third Day

We have in a previous chapter noted Mark's use of conflict and conflict stories.[1] Through them he advances the story of Jesus, he builds up the drama, and he intensifies the expectation of the reader. It should come as no surprise then to discover that on the third day he places Jesus in the temple, and this time he puts him in direct conflict with the temple voices and authorities. The battle has been building ever since the opening of the Gospel. It has intensified in the first two visits to the temple. Now it reaches the level of confrontation. There are some parallels and some differences between this series of conflict stories and the earlier grouping, and these are worthy of note.

In the early series the conflict was directed by the scribes, the Pharisees and the Herodians. Now however it is directed by the elders, the Sadducees and the chief priests. This represents a subtle shift, for the latter grouping are more specifically the representatives of the religious viewpoint.[2] This conflict is directed then at a more priestly, conservative and cultic group. The earlier series had a very complex arrangement in which the central story held the others in balance. Here the stories are more like a parade of viewpoints that are presented in quick succession. Each group comes to Jesus with their issue, their question, their vested interest. For the Pharisees, who, it should be noted, are sent by the Sadducees, etc. it is the tax problem. For the Sadducees themselves, who only emerge from hiding when the Pharisees fail, it is the resurrection problem. For the scribes it is the legal problem of the great commandment.

Each of the stories shows us the vested interest of the group that comes to Jesus, but it also reveals the lack of interest by these groups in Jesus himself. The two meet looking at each other out of different eyes. Jesus sees them, and tries to respond to them as people, inviting them beyond their restricted viewpoint and their own egocentric concerns. They on the other hand do not manifest interest in him at all. He is in fact the object of their violence, not the subject of their relational interest. They are, we are told, out to "trap" him. This trapping maneuver gives a violent note to the stories, which, because of it, are clouded by an atmosphere of suspicion and hostility. Jesus by his very presence is a threat, and so his freedom must be contained. In the end however he prevails. Not only does he avoid their carefully plotted traps and slick attempts at manipulation, but, in the end, he returns to them the question they wish to avoid. He faces them with his own subjectivity. Who is he? This is the question, and this they must answer. In this he is summoning them to a whole new level of existence, and it is the ripples of uncertainty between the continuous and the discontinuous that jars and threatens them, for, as Regis Duffy puts it, "when tension between the continuity of our experience and the shock of discontinuity can no longer be avoided we are forced to decisions and choices."[3]

Another point of comparison that emerges between these stories and the earlier conflict stories is that here the issues are more related to meaning than to behavior. Granted the connection between the two, there is nonetheless a difference between them. In the earlier stories the emphasis seemed to be on the behavior itself, whether it was eating on the sabbath, or with sinners, or picking corn, etc. A change in behavior at that point might have resolved the conflict. Now the battle has been joined at a deeper level, and it is clearly now a battle of and for meaning. It is a conflict about ultimates. This matches our experience. Once the question of death invades our consciousness, once we begin to come to grips with it, the whole question of meaning is then the issue. The conflict questions and probes not just our behavior but the underlying assumptions of our lives. It challenges the accepted meaning and requests of us a new pledge and commitment to the emergent new horizon that evolves out of the conflict. Conflicts are then, as Erickson observed, "moments of decision between integration and retardation, and therefore they are critical steps and turning points."[4] These conflicts open up a new question for disciples and for us. The decisive question for man, says Chardin, is: "Is he related to something infinite or not? This is the telling question of his life."[5] It is also the telling question of these stories that occur on the third day when Jesus enters into the old temple and confronts it in its symbols of authority, power, etc., and then leaves to take up a new position opposite the old temple.

The First Conflict Story (11:27–33). This story tells of Jesus being approached by the scribes, the elders, and the chief priests. They want to know on whose authority he is acting in cleansing the temple. At the outset this is an apparently simple situation. It involves what appears to be an innocent question about authority, but behind it there is the attempt to catch Jesus in a trap. All the parties who compose the Sanhedrin are present. These are the resident powers of the temple. The debate is about authority. They have however a vested interest in the question. Their authority, their goals, their power, their purposes are at stake. They move not to gain information but to protect themselves. They have achieved a position which both requires and enables them to be the chief authorities on law and its interpretation, and on liturgy and its practice. In fact these are the very strengths that have enabled them to continue and preserve the sense of nationalistic worship since the time of Moses. Now, however, as the dialogue between Jesus and them unfolds, we see this strength dissipate in weakness.

The dialogue offers us two sets of questions. The first is offered by the members of the Sanhedrin. In response Jesus asks another question, and as Schweizer points out, "the way his question is formulated in the Greek text clearly indicates he expects an unequivocal answer."[6] The inability of his questioners to answer exposes their own weakness. It shows that they are broken in their religious faith. "The question was asked so that they might receive the kind of faith which no longer requires any proof. This may not be an accurate description of the thinking of the enemies of Jesus, yet it is very appropriate for the subject around which the conversion revolves. They cannot deny the work of God. They do not wish to be irreligious so they insist they do not know."[7]

The inner dynamics of the story are relatively simple. The representatives of the Sanhedrin move to question Jesus' authority to cleanse the temple, etc. The authority in question then is neither legal nor political; his authority is from God.[8] Jesus' counter-question returns to them their own dilemma. He asks about John's baptism which places them on the defensive and exposes their own real lack of interest in the question. They must now either convict themselves of a lack of faith or be convicted by the people for not recognizing John. The voice of the past, John the Baptist, joins with the voice of the present in exposing the voice that is not interested in meaning at all, only in its own interests.

In terms of a story of the self the resident powers correspond to something within me. They echo a part of me with which I have become familiar. Death has challenged and shaken this foundation of my way of being. The very strengths of my life, the very style of living that has got me this far, is undermined by contact with the ever present returning question. The meeting of these two raises the question of meaning and ultimacy. Why go through death? Why not try to avoid it? Why bother with it? The reality of death, as Becker and others indicate, is denied. There is a last-ditch effort to overthrow the intrusion. By what authority does meaning raise the question of relevance? Aren't things all right the way they are now? The strengths of the past become traps against the future. We must be continually letting go of the strengths of another time, of the achievements of the past, and acquiring what we need for the future. Paul Tournier speaks of the "anxiety neurosis of the middle way" as an anxiety that possesses someone who is caught between a past that is no longer appropriate and a future which the person has not yet clung to or grasped. There is, he says, "a place that must be left before we can find a new place, and in between there is a place without a place, a place without support, a place which is not a place, since a true place is support. . . . In between there comes that middle of the way anxiety."[9]

The question of the Sanhedrin reflects a consciousness that sees itself as the central and pivotal point of the whole universe. They move only to the satisfaction of their own needs, the fulfillment of their own goals, the protection of their own interests. The answer of Jesus springs from a deeper region. His answer reflects an attempt to place himself in context, first of all in context with his tradition but also in context with the whole world and with its ultimate goal. Teilhard speaks of three types of men in the universe: (a) the tired for whom existence is a mistake or a failure and who can consequently only achieve happiness by the attainment of a minimum of thought, feeling and desire; (b) the pleasure seekers (hedonists) who want only to enjoy the present moment and who refuse to risk anything for the sake of, or on the chance of the future; for them happiness is feeling good, and the goal of life is not to act and create, but to make use of opportunities; (c) the enthusiast for whom living is an ascent and a discovery; for him happiness is a by-product of the effort of forging ahead and attaining the fullness and finality of his own self. For Teilhard people can only be themselves if they are (a) centered upon their own person, (b) de-centered on the other, and (c) super-centered upon a being greater than themselves. And so Teilhard frames what he calls the triple beatitude; first be, then love, and finally worship.[10]

The story opens us to the battle between our own personal meaning and universal meaning. It is the exposure of the war of meanings and authorities. What the Sanhedrin initially seek is an external authority, a proof that permits action. What Jesus does by his response is return them to an interior authority, to a personal meaning and to the values they themselves believe in. Finally what he does with his action, cleansing the temple, etc., is to confront them with universal meaning. In the process he confronts them with the tired, hedonic and enthusiastic dimensions of their own existence.

The Second Conflict Story (12:13–17). In this story Jesus is presented with a problem: Should we pay taxes to Caesar or not? In response Jesus notes that what belongs to Caesar should be given to Caesar and what belongs to God should be given to God. This is the Pharisees' question, and again it involves a trap. Jesus by his response confronts both the questioners and Caesar not only with the possibility but also with the reality of God. He avoids the trap and in turn makes them confront reality.

The Pharisees' question was carefully designed to corner Jesus. They did not wish to deal with his own subjectivity. This is a pure political power play. Their action poses a problem. His response demands subjectivity. He says, in effect, that it all depends on who you are and what you see. If the question you ask does not incorporate the questioner, that's one thing; if it does, that's another. If the question only asks who belongs to Caesar without dealing with whom Caesar belongs to, you will get a very different answer. Caesar belongs to God. And that makes all the difference. Caesar's rule is temporal and limited. God is eternal. Caesar's world and Caesar's rule for all its apparent vastness and importance is small and puny when seen in the larger context. By contrast the individual's decision, which appears to be small and insignificant, is in the larger context momentous and important.

Viktor Frankl points out that everyone has a need for personal meaning in life and that without this man will be neurotic. He will be aimless and directionless, lacking a sense of responsibility. His meaning however appears in the concrete and not in the abstract. It is in the situation of life that he finds himself. Thus, says Frankl, man's "meaning orientation turns into meaning confrontation." It is at this point that freedom becomes responsible "before something, or to something, be it society, humanity, mankind, or his own conscience."[11] There is then a tension in man between what Frankl calls personal and universal meaning, and this conflict must be harmonized.

In the story Jesus is calling his questioners to that harmony and balance. They come with a one–dimensional viewpoint, a problem. He opens them to a larger viewpoint, to mystery. Their question is directed at coercion, to get him to conform to the expectations of political power, to implement the passed-on "collective meaning." This is designed to move him from personal meaning. His response seeks an awareness of the personal meaning of their own lives and opens them to universal meaning. Between the collective and the universal lies the personal, and it is gained through reflective awareness.

The story exposes me to a side of myself that is calculating and tricky. I know how to ask questions that seek to avoid answers. I know how to approach meaning so that it cannot answer. I know how to keep life as a problem rather than face it as mystery. It is easy for me to act impulsively and with limited data because I only want my own needs met and satisfied. The more I know, the more I am reflective, the larger my horizon, the more complex and agonizing are the decisions. I have my commitments all worked out so as to avoid any deeper commitment. Rendering to Caesar in an uncritical manner puts him in a position that is not rightfully his. The story confronts me with my "Caesar" that would rule politically, seeking only what is advantageous to its own rule. It confronts me with the accusers in me who can play Caesar off against anyone else for their own gain. It invites me to dialogue with the Christ-self that summons me from my own myopic vision to a horizon where all things belong to God. The story calls me from my restrictive, frightened and protective shell to a horizon of hope for all mankind.

The Third Conflict Story (12:18–24). This story involves his opponents coming to Jesus to ask him a question about the after-life. They pose the problem like this: If a man because of his obedience to the law has married his dead brother's wife, at the resurrection whose wife is she then to be considered? This story is called the Sadducees' question.[12] During the course of the story there is once again the attempt to trap Jesus. The story really involves two questions, one of them relating to the resurrection and the other relating to marriage. Hultgren[13] sees that the controlling question is the one relating to the resurrection. The Sadducees did not consider the doctrine of the resurrection to be based on Scripture. In their view the Pentateuch was the Scripture, and so they refused to accept as authentic and authoritative the writings of Isaiah and Daniel in which the resurrection is mentioned. Their question about marriage then is designed to show the weakness and the absurdity of the teaching on the resurrection.[14] Inherent then in this question is an attempt by Mark to deal with people's certainty about how God acts on the one hand and the freedom for God to act any way he wants on the other. The conflict, therefore, it appears, is between God's will and man's effort, between what man can do and what God does, between theology and revelation. The Sadducees were trying to get Jesus to admit that the law about Levirite marriage was basically incompatible with a teaching on resurrection. This of course was a trap in which they hoped to snare him.

Jesus does not take the bait, or rather he takes the opportunity once again to invite them to a larger vision. He says that life cannot be boxed in. You cannot restrict it to the past. You cannot contain it in law. You cannot sum it up once and for all in tradition. It cannot be encapsulated. Life breaks out. No moment in life is like any other. Each moment is new, is a surprise, is a new creation. Each moment is its own gift and brings with it the wonder of that time. Every moment must be attended to and received. Our assumptions are only that, our expectations are only that, and they must bend before the evidence of the new working of God. In his response Mark shows how God shatters our expectations. Jesus breaks through our preconceptions and presents the Kingdom of God breaking in through the unexpected.[15]

The confrontation with the returning question of death leads us to an apparent absurdity, as surely as the question of Levirite marriage. It was the death of the spouses that enabled the Pharisees to frame their question. Death also as a question brings us to the absurdity of suicide. If death is inevitable, why not accept it now? In fact why not create it? If death leads us to a future, why not now bring it about through our own power? If a death does not lead to a future, why go on? Death leads us to the absurdity of living as living leads us to the absurdity of death. The Gospel story raises both of these time-bound stories into a different dimension. Jesus opens us to a new sense of time, God's time, for in God's time everything is surprise, everything is new. God has always been coming, and nevertheless he is yet to come.[16] There is always more ahead. The now whose very presence is death, is terminal, is already past with its coming, is not all. The self exposes a life not yet lived, a vision still to be appropriated. There is a God who comes. Time itself redeemed by the self who comes in time, calls through time, and leads us out beyond the time that is now. Under the chaos at the surface there is a self, under the finality of the past there is future, under the ultimacy of death there is resurrection. There is another dimension that speaks through the self. The self that I am is a self of the living not of the dead, because the God in whose image I

am is a God of the living. In the story the Pharisees and
Sadducees are themselves aspects of me. I see them as the
counterpart of time asking the time-bound questions. Time
is the great destroyer, and everything is lost unless there is
something that comes to validate time. What saves time
that so ruthlessly destroys everything else? Only a story
larger than time. Only a story of self. Only a story of God.[17]

   The Fourth Conflict Story (12:28–34). This story concerns the scribal inquiry of Jesus relative to which is the
greatest commandment of all. Schweizer calls this "the real
question." In the story we see the same pattern as in the
others. Once again there is the question, once again the
trap, once again the conflict, and once again the return of
the question to the questioners inviting them to a larger
world of meaning. It was customary to see the love of God
and the love of man as the two great commandments. The
question now posed attempts to distinguish between them,
and, by getting Jesus to make this choice, to trap him. It
fails.

   Schweizer notes that Jesus' answer is an invitation to
his questioners "to take the final step which leads from 'not
far from' to 'into the Kingdon of God.'"[18] In response Jesus
joins together both the love of God and the love of man,
both the story of God and the story of man. For as John
Dunne says, "God is the unknown in a story of man, while
man is the unknown in a story of God."[19] Jesus begins by
quoting the Shema, the creed, which every Israelite recited,
and he joins to it the passage from Leviticus 19:18 on the
love of neighbor. The inclusive nature of Christ's response
is of enormous value. He is transcending any separateness.
He is pointing to the unitary nature of existence. The implication of this response is seen in the writings of de Chardin
and in our time is being continued through the work of
Thomas Berry at the Riverdale Center for Religious

Research. Both believe deeply in the idea of an evolving world and in a religious viewpoint that is creation-oriented instead of redemption-oriented (as its fundamental emphasis). Berry states three principles which lie at the center of this thrust, and they can be articulated as follows:

A. "Law of Differentiation" which states there is variety in everything and that this variety has been brought about by the earth. Diversity and plurality, differentiation and multiplicity are part of the stuff of life. Now in man that differentiation is a choice.

B. "Law of Subjectivity" which says that things are only different because at their center they are inviolate and therefore irreplaceable and totally holy. To deprive any being of the sacred quality is to disrupt the total order of the universe.

C. "Law of Intercommunion" which says that everything mutually indwells. The universe binds the whole, and nothing falls apart, and in man this law is the law of love.[20]

The response that Jesus gives to his questioners not only shows the unitary nature of existence but the totality of the response required. The whole person must respond. It requires heart, and soul, mind and strength, a quaternity that reflects wholeness and totality. The mind is the organ commonly associated with knowledge, and in the Bible to "know" someone is synonymous with loving acceptance, mutuality, and intimacy. To know someone is to penetrate to the depths of the other as person. Strength in the Bible is often referred to as the capacity to act with justice. God's hand is strong, his right hand is filled with justice, and he will act on behalf of his people. Thus to love with strength involves the "doing of the deeds" of justice and righteousness. To love with your heart is a third dimension that Scripture speaks of frequently. The heart is the seat of affections. It is the place of appreciation and memory, of receptivity and acceptance. To love with the heart then is to love graciously, warmly, affectionately. Finally Jesus tells them to love with the "soul," a term difficult to translate but perhaps that can be described as "with spirit"; they are to have a spirit of love, an élan about them, a willingness to believe in the goodness of others and in their possibilities.

In terms of a story of the self there is here then a dialogue between Jesus and the scribes in me. The scribes correspond to something in me that is in many ways fundamentally isolationistic and competitive. It seeks to discover which is the best part of me. It plays upon a dual understanding of my own nature and has a tendency to divide people into good parts and bad parts, into acceptable and unacceptable parts. It starts from a basis of inferiority, poor self-image, etc. It not only isolates me from others but also tends to isolate me from myself. Jesus on the other hand is the self that invites me to love out of totality, to love generously and openly, to enlarge my vision to embrace a wider cosmos in terms of self, other and God. The self calls me to a trinitarian connectedness wherein all things and people are different, where all is sacred and holy, and it invites me to see that this is so precisely because all things are related.

The Fifth Conflict Story (12:35–37). This story contains what Schwiezer calls "the decisive question." Here Jesus asks the scribes and Pharisees the question which apparently has to do with the Davidic descent of the Messiah. He asks, "If the Messiah is David's son, how can David himself call him Lord?" It is significant that here

Jesus initiates the closing dialogue just as he did in the first series of stories (cf. 3:1–6). The flow of energy, the movement of this last question, is from the center to the periphery, from Jesus to the listeners. The whole tenor of the story shows it to be the climactic question. Hultgren indicates that here "there are no opponents and there is no closing pronouncement" to the story and that therefore there is no conflict. The question that Jesus asks he sees as a rhetorical one.[21] The question certainly hangs in the air; it awaits an answer from everyone. It is not rhetorical in the sense that no one need answer it. Everyone must. The Gospel has been demanding the answer throughout all its stories. There is in Jesus' question clearly a question of identity: Whose son is he?

Ever since the centerpoint of the Gospel this question has become more pronounced. There Jesus was addressed by Bartimaeus as Son of David but no further comment was given. The question was in effect being brought forward by the outsider Bartimaeus. Now the question is being moved from within. David was the singer of psalms who proclaimed that the Messiah to come would be his Lord. In raising the question of his own identity with them in the manner that he did, Jesus is doing an interesting thing. He returns them to their guiding image, David, and by doing that shows that the guiding image is itself a testimony to one who is greater, who is to come. He returns them to their own question and affirms it as question. It was only in discovering that, or, better still, in rediscovering that question, that they would begin to perceive the greater mystery toward which he was opening them.

In terms of a story of the self this rings true. There is no moment at which I am not being addressed. The self that I am at the center, the self that leads me into the unknown, that calls me into contact with all of life and all of reality,

ultimately summons me to name myself as mystery. Who I
am cannot be stated apart from who God is. I am returned
by life itself to the guiding images of my life. Life experiences and death experiences precipitate a search for meaning which returns us to our guiding images. They witness
to life itself and to its personal center. In returning the people to the image of David Jesus is effectively showing them
how David himself longed for more, sought something
beyond his own limited experience. David was himself in
search of the Messiah whom he called Lord. This guiding
image for the people pointed to something else that was to
come. Jesus is that something else. He is superior to David.
He is the Son of God.

At the conclusion of the conflict stories Jesus leaves the
temple for the last time (13:1). He now assumes a new position on the Mount of Olives. His disciples ask him to look
over at the temple. Their insinuation is: How beautiful it is!
They see, however, only its beauty in terms of its concrete
reality. There is much that they fail to see. They do not see
the new cornerstone, they do not perceive the new temple
among them, they do not intuit the new hymn of praise,
and this is tragic. These disciples have been with him all
through the Gospel and they fail to see. Their concern is for
the end—the end of the temple, the end of history, the end
of their known world. What, they want to know, will be the
sign, and when will it happen? Characteristically this is a
semitic way of asking one question. Their concern is for the
end, and it contrasts sharply with his concern, because he
is obviously preoccupied with the new temple and the
emergent time of God.

Here in Chapter 13 there is another one of those frames
that highlight Mark's Gospel. In 13:5–6 there is a warning
about false prophets, and again this is mentioned in 13:21–
22. Who are these people? They are, we are informed, to be

marked with "signs and wonders." They are a charismatic group of people who are noted for their joy, enthusiasm and fervor. Sometimes they got carried away so that it was hard to tell whether they themselves were the Lord. They were noted for pursuing the miraculous and the extraordinary. Mark does not look favorably on them and is insistent that seeing Jesus' miracles is not enough, observing his activities is insufficient, hearing his teachings is not the ultimate. He wants the disciples to see more than the "wise teacher, the compassionate friend, the worker of wonders."[22] He warns his listeners that Jesus is coming back and they must therefore be careful not to subscribe too easily to the position of the *theos andres*, the wonder workers, who deceive people into thinking he has returned.

The community therefore is to be watchful. This is the key. The end is not end. This is but the beginning of the birth pangs. The disciples must be willing to endure much more suffering, and then the end will come, but nobody knows the exact time. The believer is not to get caught up in the kind of endless and unproductive speculation. Mark "deliberately wards off a strongly apocalyptic expectation of an immediate end, and he summons the Church to be watchful."[23]

In terms of the story of self, then, these three days, together with their conflict stories, allow us to see the gradual movement toward confrontation with, and replacement of, the temple. There is a warning against the expectation that this is the end, or against speculation as to when the end will come. We are warned against the dangers of signs and wonders and false prophets and admonished to be watchful and to stay awake. The emergence of the new center, of the more conscious religious sense, flows from the entry into the quiet. And it is frequently a two-edged sword as Thomas Mann has noted, "Solitude gives birth to the original in us, to beauty unfamiliar and perilous ... to poetry. But also it gives birth to the opposite, to the perverse, the illicit, the absurd."[24] The spirits must indeed be tested, as the great mystics remind us, lest in the new moment a regression, a forgetfulness occurs and leads us back to the old attractions, miracles, wonders and signs. This is the real danger.[25]

Chapter 16
Absence and Presence

The passion story in St. Mark's Gospel is set within a typical Markan frame.[1] Here the stories that constitute the frame involve women. The first is the incident of the anonymous woman who anoints Jesus in 14:3–9. Tradition has given her the name of Mary. The second concerns the women who came to the tomb to anoint him in 16:1–8. The two stories have similar colorings; both mention women, both mention anointing, and both mention the absence of Christ. In the first story it is Jesus himself who draws attention to his absence by saying, "I shall not always be with you" (v. 7), and in the second story the announcement is made by the young man sitting inside the tomb: "He is not here. He has been raised. Look, here is the place where they laid him" (16:6).

There are many surprises in the story of the anonymous woman who anoints Jesus. What is surprising "is that she (Mary) breaks into the company of men and suddenly anoints Jesus during the meal . . . and not before it."[2] What is surprising is that Mark notes the fact that she anoints his head, while in John we are told that she anointed his feet

(Jn 12:3). What is surprising is that Jesus interprets the anointing himself. He sees it as a woman doing a "beautiful thing for me. . . . She poured perfume on my body to prepare it for burial ahead of time" (vv. 6–8). What is surprising is that while it evokes another anointing ceremony, the Davidic anointing, it contrasts sharply with it in the very moment it brings it to mind. In fact Kelber goes so far as to say: "It dramatically reverses all aspects of the Davidic ceremony. He is not anointed in the temple but at his place outside of and opposite to Jerusalem and its temple. His is not a celebration in royal glitter and priestly pomp but a table fellowship in the house of a leper. He is not anointed by the priests or the high priest but by an anonymous woman. His anointment is not applauded but criticized. Above all he is not anointed to power and life but beforehand for burial."[3]

The identity of the woman who does the anointing is debated. This is attributable to a comparison with the other Gospels. In Luke 7:36–50 the woman is identified only as a sinner, while in John 12:1–8 she is called Mary of Bethany. Further differences arise when one compares the stories, for in John and Luke the feet of Jesus are anointed whereas in Matthew (26:6–13) and Mark the head is anointed. Whether there were one or two anointings therefore is unclear. What is quite clear is the meaning of the event which is supplied by Jesus himself: "She poured perfume on my body to prepare it ahead of time for burial" (v. 8). Jesus was so moved by this that he promised that this moment, this event, would be spoken of "wherever the Gospel is preached." It would not be forgotten.

In the second part of the frame at the other end of the passion (16:1) there is again the sharpness of surprise. If in the first story the woman is anonymous and alone, here she is named and multiple. There is the surprise at finding the women at the tomb. Why did they go to anoint him? Was not this already accomplished at Bethany? Schweizer finds their presence there "very strange." And he also finds somewhat strange the sudden ending of 16:8 when they "went out and ran from the grave in fear and terror and said nothing to anyone because they were afraid."[4] Further surprises are part of the story itself. The women are "stunned" at the discovery that the stone has been rolled away. They are surprised by the voice of the young man, but, more than anything else, there is the shock that Jesus is absent. The tomb has been opened without human intervention, and this is highlighted by Mark in that he draws our attention to the size of the stone; it was, he says, "very big."

The women then that form the frame are interesting, and they are important in considering both discipleship and the passion story which they hold together. In the first story the woman who anoints Jesus has clearly been enabled to hear his message. She is obviously approving him and accepting him in his going to death, in his absence. She is moved to do this "something extravagant" for him. She goes out from herself to him. She has become alive to the fact of his death. She has intuited this and moves toward him. She takes with her a jar of oil. In fact Mark is careful to point out that it was "an alabaster jar full of very expensive perfume made of pure nard" and he stresses it a second time by pointing out how the people are angry and upset at "wasting" this expensive perfume. Mary, if that be her name, is indeed doing an extraordinary thing. She is finding meaning in the midst of the meaningless. She makes sense out of what appears to be the senseless death of Jesus. All of the other disciples found reasons for either avoiding or denying it. Where rationalization, intellectualization and denial fail, loving, intuitive, acceptance succeeds. Mary expresses this meaning in the ritual anointing and through it expresses faith in the value of life. Mary knows what to hold on to and what to let go of, what is necessity and what is merely dressing, what is peripheral and what is central.[5]

As a disciple Mary demonstrates greatness. She expresses a capacity to embrace the dying Jesus. She can receive him in his presence but also in his absence. She can entertain absence and presence as part of the mystery of life, and in the anointing of oil she is conferring all of its symbolic qualities to him. Oil feeds the flame of light, nourishes the body, relieves pain. It is light and food and medicine. In anointing him she is manifesting true discipleship. Henri Nouwen, speaking of absence and presence, observes that "the mystery of God's presence can be touched only by a deep awareness of his absence. It is in the center of our longing for the absent God that we discover his footprints and realize that our desire to love God is born out of the love with which he has touched us. In the patient waiting for the loved one we discover how much he has filled our lives already. . . . By listening to our longings we hear God as their Creator."[6] Mary listened, Mary heard, Mary responded.

Mary is willing to let go, it appears. She is willing to accept his entrance into death. She corresponds to something in me that can gradually come to accept, to receive death as part of life. It is such an essential task, but the surprising thing is that it is possible. One can accept, one can let go. The difficulty of the task is well attested, but so is its possibility. The feminine in me wants to make contact, to bring to the resources of my person her capacity to receive, to nourish, to affirm, to accept, at a new and deeper level. She wishes not so much to overturn the masculine structures of my existence as to balance them, but to do this there is a side of me that must relinquish and let go. For the journey to go forward you have to let go of where you've been, what you have accomplished, what you have achieved. Otherwise you cannot live more fully, or, as Walter Burghardt puts it, "loss is heaped on loss, indignity on indignity, social, psychic, physical and intellectual. . . . What is left is not what I have achieved, not what I have amassed; what is left is who I am."[7]

The themes of absence and presence are also very much a part of the Last Supper scene, and here it becomes even more evident that there is need to integrate the essential ambivalence of life if we are to be whole. This of course is a theme that runs throughout Jung's writings also. The supper begins with the relatively innocent question: "Where will you have us go and prepare for you to eat the Passover?" Clearly the supper intended in the question is the Passover supper. The meal that is celebrated however is not a Passover meal. Many of the elements of such a meal are absent. The lamb is not eaten, the Passover liturgy is not recited, the words of explanation do not conform to the normal form that was customary at Passover and they do not appear at the same point in the meal.[8] What kind of meal is this that Jesus is having with the disciples? He has many meals with the disciples and others, and while these have a greater prominence in Luke's Gospel they are nonetheless of equal importance in Mark. At times these meals were shared with disciples, at times with sinners. Sometimes he is guest of honor at the meal, sometimes the host. At times he even switches roles; he is invited as a guest and ends up as the host. The meals then are significant. It appears that more than eating and drinking was going on when they came together to dine. This is further borne out by the presence of conflict at all the Markan meals. It began in Chapters 2 and 3 when the Pharisees and Herodians end up joining forces to plot his death. It continued in the eating stories of Chapters 6 and 8 when the disciples are advised to beware of the leaven of the Pharisees. It comes to the fore again now as they sit at this last meal at which the ingredients are conflict, betrayal and suspicion. "Is it I, Lord?" reflects much of the mood of the meal.

Mark is a careful author. We have noticed this before. And now we see again the care with which he approaches this meal. He patterns the description of the preparation for Eucharist on the entry into Jerusalem[9] and then describes this meal in the same way as the other meals. Mark has Jesus use the same formula as in the other meals. He "takes," "blesses," "breaks," and "gives" the bread and wine to those who are gathered, but there is one big difference in this meal. He does not give equal attention to the bread and wine. "Only fifteen Greek words are used by Mark to describe the blessing, distribution and interpretation of the bread; in contrast fifty-one words are devoted to the thanksgiving, distribution, and interpretation of the cup.[10] Is there a reason for this unequal emphasis? Robbins sees that the bread is subservient to the cup which evokes the crucifixion and absence of Jesus as a corrective to those who think that sitting at a meal telling of the miracles of Jesus is sufficient.[11] The meal then is an invitation into the cup of suffering.

In this meal Jesus is stressing a counterbalance to the values that tend to dominate the disciples' thinking, namely strength, power, miracles, popularity, money, position, etc. Instead of these he places before them weakness, littleness, kindness and poverty. These are being given a special emphasis and dignity. Mark has therefore little of the comforts of the other Gospels in his Last Supper. Jesus does not speak of his love for them, he does not promise the Spirit, etc., as in John, he does not exhibit the same desire to eat the meal with them as he does in Luke where there are great elements of celebration as well as darkness, and where Jesus prays for Peter and the disciples, etc. Here the meal is marked with heavy colors, and what seems to be stressed is the separation, the suffering, the absence. If indeed, says Robbins, "some members of the community invoke the presence of Jesus through their eating, Mark stands this on its head through this scene which announces his absence."[12]

Absence and presence seem to be a rhythm all through the Gospel. Jesus' leaving and Jesus' coming back is a flow of energy in the Markan story. Each moment of absence seems to be followed by a more intense moment of presence. When he has been with them for a while they begin to take him for granted and create an illusion about themselves. They elevate their status, position and importance. Their identity becomes inflated. In the moments of darkness there is a reversal, and in the experience of his absence they are invited to a new awareness. Both the anointing and the Last Supper witness to this truth. The disciples want to accept a non-suffering center, a non-suffering Christ, and then they can maintain the celebrative joviality and convivial bliss of dining together. Jesus however insists that there is an experience of absence which comes and which manifests a suffering God, and they are invited to it. This experience of absence is the invitation to an exchange of life, for in the moment that he speaks of his absence and the cup of suffering, he also offers them food, and, as Haughton says, food is a kind of communication, and to give and to receive food is to exchange life.[13]

What is the net effect of this absence-presence cycle? The disciples learn differentiation. They are not identical with Christ. They are disciples. His absence is for their benefit. What he offers them is a relationship with him and an identification with him, a relationship that will support, sustain, and strengthen them. Nouwen puts it succinctly when he observes that "in the center of our sadness for his absence we can find the first signs of his presence, and in the middle of our longings we discover the footprints of the one who created them."[14]

Chapter 17
Gethsemani

In Chapter 14 Mark's Jesus comes to the garden of Gethsemani, a place that has become both famous and infamous throughout Christendom. This garden is well named, for Gethsemani means "oil press." It is a very appropriate place, therefore, for the kind of events that happen there on that night. Jesus comes to the garden with the disciples. Three times he leaves them and returns to invite them to be with him but he finds them asleep. Finally Judas comes and betrays him, and Jesus is left alone with his captors as everyone flees. At the center of the story we see again evidence of Mark's technique for intensifying the drama and catching our attention as he gives us an event in triplicate.

Gethsemani is a story that functions on many levels. It is crucial to the development of the Gospel as a whole, it has a special place within the passion, and yet it stands as a story on its own. As such it has an intensity and significance of its own in which we witness the development of both Christ and the disciples. The movement of Christ in the story alternates between two poles. This has been true all through the Gospel but it is more evident here. On the

161

one hand he moves in prayer to the Father, entering into silence and aloneness to communicate with him. On the other hand he moves in care and friendship toward his disciples. Both movements need to be explored, for they reflect both a sense of urgency and the central concern of his life. This dynamic energy is what gives Gethsemani its crushing and enervating significance on the one hand and its hope and life on the other.

Looking at the first of these poles, then, we see that Gethsemani is a place where the care and affection of Jesus for the apostles is manifested. The apostles have been with Jesus and seen the many acts that he performed and that reflected his power and glory. They have been impressed by this and it has captured their attention. Now it is the apostles and not Jesus who must undergo trial, and Gethsemani, says Kelber,[1] is where we see this temptation. They had failed to hear the "returning question" of death and suffering on three occasions, and now in Gethsemani they sleep on three occasions. As the first three moments underscored their failure to be attentive to the question, so now their failure to stay awake underscores even more the dimension of their failure. You could perhaps excuse them falling asleep, once but when it happens three times and you are aware of Mark's use of events in threes, then you cannot miss the significance of it.[2]

Gethsemani then, viewed from this vector, is the story of Jesus' awakening to their falling asleep. It is his discovery that he stands alone and that he can expect and indeed receive very little help from the group. Yet he cares. Three times he interrupts his own prayer to go to them and to call them to participate in the process by remaining awake and watchful. It is interesting to note the point made by Kelber that from now on in Mark's Gospel Jesus will not call Peter by that name again. He reverts to calling him Simon, as indeed John has Jesus also do after the death in Chapter 21 of his Gospel. This reversal is significant, for "the bestowal of the new name at the appointment of the twelve had signaled Peter's ascendancy to leadership, so the one and only recurrence of the old name signifies his demotion."[3] Peter will sink even deeper as the passion progresses, and the three sleeping moments that he encounters now in the company of others will give way to three denials which he will have to endure alone.

Gethsemani is then very much a story of Jesus and the apostles. It is also a story of Jesus and the Father. As we switch our attention to this vector we see Jesus in prayer.[4] He has already been portrayed in this stance in the Gospel. He prayed at Capernaum (1:35), he is seen in prayer following the feeding of the five thousand (6:45), he is seen in prayer here in Gethsemani and finally we will meet him in prayer on the cross (15:34). The content of his prayer here reflects the point we have already made, his love for the apostles. Mark concentrates on the prophecy of Zechariah: "I will strike the shepherd and the sheep will be scattered" (Zech 13:7). His prayer is for the flock, for the apostles, that they be spared the trial he is undergoing. His prayer reflects the minimization of his own suffering and emphasizes his care for the apostles.

In this prayer Jesus does not invite the apostles to pray with him. This is something he does alone. He takes them with him from the supper, he invites them to the garden, but once they are in the garden they seem to have their place and he has his, and at least in Mark they are not invited to that space. The command is even more emphasized in Matthew where Jesus says, "You stay here while I go over there to pray." The "here" is very clearly in opposition to the "there" where the apostles' position is to be.[5] The prayer then in the garden is a conversation for Jesus alone: it is time for him and his Father to be in communion. There is a need for him to be in tune with the Father.

Jesus encounters what Sebastian Moore calls the blank as he goes to the apostles and finds them asleep and then comes to the Father and finds him very quiet and silent. Abba is now apparently absent or at least not manifestedly present. As he encounters the blank he seems to become more and more troubled. In this sense there is some development. The "sudden fear that comes over him and great distress" quickly seem to go through a second wave of anguish. The fear becomes a "sorrow in my heart that is so great it nearly crushes me." Shortly after that a third phase is reached as Jesus "went a little further on, threw himself on the ground and prayed that if possible he might not have to go through this hour." It is here in this movement that Jesus enters into the blank, the void, this apparent absence of Abba, this awful lonely quiet and comes to the realization that God is not Abba as he understood Abba.

Moore calls the "blank" the "gateway to the interior, to our inner space, which is infinite," and in commenting on T.S. Eliot's *Four Quartets* he notices that the blank has four faces, each corresponding to one of the quartets. There is, he says, the blank in knowledge contemplated in serene philosophical detachment which he finds in "Burnt Norton." There is the blank history in the endless succession of generations that he finds in "East Coker." In "Dry Salvages" the blank is discovered in the elemental non-human rhythms that pulsate in us. Finally in "Little Gidding" the blank is transformed by Pentecostal fire. The blank here is similar to the experience of nothingness we have previously described, and yet this episode in Gethsemani is only its beginning. The blank deepens all through the passion. Here there is, at least initially, a kind of struggling and resistance to it. In fact in the passion narrative, until his arrest in 14:43,

Jesus is very much in control. He is the constant activator. He initiates the action, even though the events being recorded are mostly affecting him. In the first part of the passion Jesus speaks thirteen times, while after 14:42 he speaks only four times and then in short cryptic statements (14:28, 62; 15:2, 34).

Gethsemani is a place of pain and sorrow for both Jesus and the disciples, and yet the response of both to the blank and the darkness is very different. One is isolationistic, the other is inclusivistic. Jesus enters into an aloneness and apartness that is different from that of the apostles. They can only handle the blank with sleep, with escape, with denial of the circumstances that form the fabric of their life. They return to the quiet of a smaller world vision each still in his own apartness. Jesus on the other hand entering the loneliness and the darkness releases its creative possibilities. They come to a womb of new birth and turn it back to a tomb of childhood; he enters a tomb of death and as we shall see converts it to a womb of possibility. Jesus seeks the meaning in spite of everything to the contrary. Their egocentric concerns which have been evident throughout the Gospel move in one direction. His heroism moves in another. They move to blot out reality, to curb the pain, to find the sleep of ignorance and the rest of oblivion; he moves toward meaning. He seeks to advance to his destiny which is inclusiveness. And so he won't give up on them. He invites them to share the moment as best they can, recognizing that they cannot be in that moment as he is, that here in confrontation with the blank they cannot lead. They can only follow.

What is the implication of this for a story of the self? There is a givenness to life that I encounter. I meet it in and through the other, the not me. I encounter this givenness in the sweep of history, the sweep of time, as I stand at a moment that is continuous with all of history and yet different from it. Time, as my memory of the past, crashes into this moment. Time as a constancy of change breaks in upon my consciousness of this moment. Time as repetition, as a cyclical succession of patterns, smashes into this moment with a consequent sense of futility. Time as possibility however also seems to be present here. The self that I am grapples with time, grapples with meaning, grapples with the givenness of life and with the sometimes apparent unfairness of it all.

I stand here in the darkness and in the blank. My ego seems to move in one direction, my self in another. As I take this story into my life it opens me to this movement in me. My normally conscious waking attitude wishes to move away from pain, wishes to move toward sleep. On the other hand I feel another stirring, a desiring in a different direction that is hardly desire, a movement toward wholeness. This drive, power, movement, yearning, this life-seeking forward thrust is personalizing. It seeks relationships and totality. It seeks to incorporate the unlived elements, that tend to sleep in fear, with the future possibilities that are sensed in the quiet, into a unified whole. As I stand in the blank, tomorrow seems to come closer to yesterday and today spans the two rather quickly. Initially the blank has all the qualities of the horizon, it fades away and draws near, it shifts and yet it is stable, it is real and yet an illusion, it is permanent and yet transitory, it is known and yet unknown. As my life progresses the blank becomes more penetrating, it hits me beyond the surface, near the core. The ego cannot deal with it; it hides in sleep and denial, for it knows that what is at issue now is everything. The successive moments of my life collapse into it, the future depends on it, and nothing else matters. I stand alone before the blank and wait. I can only receive in this place and I wonder if life is ultimately unconcerned and uncaring or caring and gracious. I alternate between coming to my sleeping, denying ego and going forth to the mystery beyond that seems to beckon.

Chapter 18
The Passion

The passion story in Mark's Gospel begins at 14:43 and runs all the way to 15:47. It is by far the longest single story piece of the Gospel. Indeed many commentators see the rest of the Gospel as a mere introduction to it.[1] The passion is a story of conflict, violence, betrayal and desertion on the one hand, and, on the other, a story of love, fidelity, and endurance. It is a journey into ever deepening darkness on a number of different levels, as we shall see, and this darkness colors the atmosphere of everything that happens. The darkness not only is something that seems to envelop Jesus, but the whole supporting cast in this dramatic scene is cast in equally heavy colors. Weeden supports a position that shows the apostles in an extremely negative light and says that Mark, having totally discredited the apostles throughout the Gospel, now shows them as "obdurate, obtuse and recalcitrant." And he closes his Gospel, therefore, without ever rehabilitating them.

In the passion story we have again a clustering of images around the central figure of Christ. These images and symbols are primordial and archetypal. On the one hand we have Jesus, the historical person, entering his death, the historical event. The story is also Jesus as symbolic light entering death as symbolic darkness. This death is the abyss whose shadows we have touched previously in the Gospel. It is the final void, the ultimate nothingness. It is indeed, as Shakespeare put it, "the undiscovered country from whose bourne no traveller returns." It is the thing, event, situation that puzzles the mind. The very words that we use to try to talk about it or describe it are themselves indicative of its significance. They are heavy words and they reflect the difficulty. We speak of such things as the abyss, the void, the depth, the emptiness, etc. This death meets us with its glaring silence and evokes turmoil, change, and finally a deafening silence. The passion, whatever else it is, is certainly Jesus entering that event.

In this story there are many characters that interact with Jesus. Some play a major role in the movement of Jesus to his death. Others figure minimally in the event. All however are part of the clustering of symbols I have alluded to earlier. Each character has what Kelber calls an "external function," that is, they represent something to the audience, symbolize realities which link up with the readers' present and serve as models of meaning and conduct.[2] What happens to them in the story is helpful in terms of trying to understand the central figure. Thus it is striking to follow the change or lack of it they undergo in the passion. The soldiers, for instance, who are so active during the scourging appear relatively indifferent and unconcerned during the death scene, the passers-by who appear to be merely observers without any vested interest in the events are unable to maintain their objectivity, the temple authorities grounded in the certainty of the Scriptures end up as the comedians of the story, while the two thieves whom one would expect to have a certain empathy with Christ and his situation end up adding to his pain, suffering, and isolation as they join in the chorus of taunts and insults. In this manner the whole world is turned upside down. There is the juxtaposition of the familiar and the strange, the known and the unknown.

This portrait of the world being turned upside down is further enhanced by the appearance of three rather unusual friends in the passion story. Simon of Cyrene is one of these. He is "a Jewish resident of Jerusalem, originally from what is today Libya and he does what none of the disciples were able to do—carry the cross after Jesus—an essential trait of discipleship."[3] So you have a non-disciple performing the act of discipleship, and then in the very midst of that his friendship with Jesus is undermined by the fact that he is forced and coerced to undertake the task. Joseph of Arimathea is likewise a friend of some complexity. On the one hand he is a member of the council that condemns Jesus to death. Nevertheless he comes to prepare Jesus for burial as a friend.

The third friend who appears in this strange story is the centurion. He is the representative of those in the adversary position. He is a Roman. Nevertheless he too does what the disciples, and particularly Peter, couldn't do. As the leader of the opposition he proclaims the identity of Jesus at the very moment Peter, the representative leader of the disciples, cannot. Again the world is turned upside down.

When we move to other elements of the passion we are again struck by the darkness. The progressive nature of the darkness adds to the sense of the world being upended. The day, which is bright and which is symbolic of consciousness, hope etc., becomes dark; the earth, which is solid and symbolic of all that is secure and safe, etc., quakes; the curtain of the temple is torn in two and the silence of Jesus is shattered with cries. This kind of physical darkness however is only the beginning. Within it other developments are shown. Mark divides the day into three-hour intervals.[4] It begins at 9 A.M. when they nailed Jesus to the cross. Then the emotional darkness began. The mockery and the taunting continued throughout the day. Mark in typical fashion mentions three groups that participated in the mockery. In v. 29 he says that "the people passing by" were in on it, in v. 31 he says that the "chief priests and the teachers of the law" had a say in it, and in v.32 he tells us that "the two crucified with him insulted him also." The emotional darkness is complete. Then Mark points out a third darkness. This is cosmic in proportions. Mark observes that the "whole country was covered with darkness which lasted for three hours." Again a reference to three, again a hint at the totality of the darkness. Finally Mark moves to spiritual darkness. At the ninth hour, three o'clock in the afternoon, there is a loud cry, "Eloi, Eloi, lama sabachthani," which means, "My God, my God, why have you abandoned me?" The darkness is final. Death arrives.

Before moving on to a consideration of Jesus as the central character in this drama it is important to say that each of the other characters is helpful for prayer and meditation. I will offer briefly then some avenues for furthering this line of action. I have borrowed liberally from both Kelber and Michie's studies while adding some reflective questions and observations of my own as I treat the six or seven major characters in the passion.

1. **Judas.** We know that he is an intimate friend of Jesus. He is a disciple and, having been selected by Jesus, now shares fellowship with him and eats with him. He is admitted to the inner circle of intimacy; he learns from Jesus and shares his vision and hope. Judas however is quite willing to use Jesus to his own advantage. He will

manipulate him if he gets a chance. Judas is very clever. He knows how to get things done. In many ways he is the most intelligent of the apostles. He knows Jesus is going to his death. He believes Jesus but figures that if he is going to die anyway there is no harm in cashing in on the moment. Jesus then becomes in Judas' eyes a something, less than a person. He becomes an object of barter, a commodity to be exchanged, a product that is dispensable for a better offer. In meditation then I am drawn to see these characteristics in my own life. What are the things in my life for which I am willing to barter my self? I might begin to catch them if I look to the things I call the golden opportunities. Scripture says, "Judas was looking for a chance." He was on the watch for it. It is also interesting and hopeful to notice the stance of Jesus. He covers for Judas, calls to him, seeks him. He wishes to reconcile Judas and to draw him back into a healing, non-betraying relationship with him. The self seeks wholeness, not fragmentation.

2. **Barrabas.** Barrabas is a character who appears to be at the other end of the scale from Judas. He is a much more physical character, much more political. He is a revolutionary who has been in trouble with the authorities many times. He refuses any cooperation with them. He must be kept behind bars. He had been arrested for a killing during a political rally. On the other hand he is like Judas in that he too is a man of violence. He however is much more up-front and physical in his approach. Barrabas is freed while Jesus is condemned. The price of his freedom is Jesus' limitation, suffering, death. What is it like to discover the murderous potential in myself? What is it like to touch my own anger? How does it feel to discover that everyone else in life is both limit and invita-

tion? Barrabas puts me in touch with my physicality and my life as limit and invitation.

3. **The High Priest.** The high priest is the representative of the official institution of religion, its laws, its rituals, its format of worship, etc. Since he shares the same faith as Jesus, we expect friendship between them. It is not the case. He seems to be determined that Jesus must die. He presses onward time after time for conviction. It is perhaps significant that in Mark, then, this trial takes place at night.[5] The high priest tries to get the world of Jesus and Rome to fit within his categories. He is so preoccupied with this that he misses the new revelation breaking in from the unknown person in front of him. It is the return of the old battle we have witnessed in the Gospel. The known friendly values I have inherited tend to resist the intrusion of the new. The priest and the prophet, the individual and the collective, the emergent and the defined clash once more. Sometimes the work we do or the insight we have which we believe might help to build, sustain and develop the Church seems to get in the way of the Church. Sometimes religious culture interferes with authentic religious freedom. It is interesting to note how in this story Jesus is the antidote to the high priest. The high priest condemns life, imprisons life, trumps up charges against life in the name of life. Jesus accepts death, accepts suffering, accepts condemnation, but is the person who advances life. The high priest ends up with death. Jesus ends up with life.

4. **Simon of Cyrene.** Simon of Cyrene is a rather innocent man, a bystander who is pressed into service and made to carry the cross. He wasn't looking for the job. He didn't really volunteer for the position. He wasn't vigi-

lantly waiting to be asked. He carries the cross without ever really knowing why. He carries it because it is forced on him. He is caught by events, by a situation which Scripture seems to indicate had very little to do with him as a person. He just happened to be there. The event broke into his life with unexpected suddenness. The normal routine of his life is crushed, broken, finished. He is confronted with possibilities. The unexpected invades the routine, the unusual invades the normal. In terms of a story of the self Simon puts me in touch with the routines of my existence and my surprising dependency on them. The tragic, comic, joyful moments of life collapse the routines if I let them. Simon asks many questions of me about my routines. What's it like for me then when tragedy breaks into my life, when the unexpected comes? What is it like to discover that now I hold a cross and I don't know why? What is it like to touch that side of us that exists somewhere between never been known and never been forgotten, and to realize that a simple but powerful thing called decision is what makes the difference?

5. **Pilate.** Pilate is the representative of secular power and prestige. He is courageous enough in that he is willing to confront the Jewish leaders.[6] At first glance he appears to be the enemy of Jesus since he is the representative of Rome, secular power, etc. He certainly stands in marked contrast to Jesus. Truth leads Pilate to question and to doubt. His world view enters upon crisis. He must either expand his horizon so as to enlarge his vision or go backward and regress to a small world. He has sensed or intuited something. He cannot with certainty condemn Jesus, but the need for popularity leads him to forget something essential about himself. He forgets that he

was made for truth, and in forgetting that he is willing to live forever with the lie which is essentially a false vision about himself, life, and the world. Pilate therefore "abdicates his judicial responsibility and turns to the crowd for a decision."[7] What is it like when I recognize that I am made for truth but that I am frequently willing to compromise that essential view about myself for the sake of popularity and social standing? What in me is social, powerful, visible, that needs constant reinforcement from people and that tends to control my life? Perhaps I can touch it if I look at my communication processes. Pilate's communication is placating in its direction.[8] He has all the signs of being a pleaser. He is sensitive to criticism, seeks constant approval, tries to read and anticipate other people's needs (notice the scourging, releasing Barrabas, etc.). He shifts from position to position easily without being grounded in anything beyond himself or within himself other than the moment. Jesus responds however in truth and in honesty. He is leveling in his communication.

6. **Joseph of Arimethea.** Joseph is another one of these passion characters. He is somewhat ambivalent. At one moment he is the friend and at another the enemy. He is a member of the Sanhedrin, and Mark carefully points out that all the members of the council condemned Jesus. He must therefore have been part of that decision-making process. On the other hand he is also the one who is willing to approach Pilate to request the body of Jesus for burial. Montague points out that his action is all the more remarkable in that he is not a relative of Jesus, yet he intercedes for one condemned for treason.[9] He is willing to risk his status and his position in coming to request Jesus' body. Thus Joseph is the one who ends up caring

for Jesus' body. He buys the shroud, wraps the body, washes it and places it in the tomb. Joseph, we may assume, had some kind of change of heart between the hearing at the trial and the death of Jesus. He seems to fit well into James Carroll's description of the prayerful person as one who is "attentive to the structures of goodness, alive to the tragic, on top of fear, ready to laugh and who is articulate in the word of God."[10] Joseph reveals a process of ascending by descending, of finding light by finding darkness.

7. **The Centurion.** The centurion is the final character I wish to comment on. He is the first person in the Gospel to make the profession of Christian faith. He comes to the realization that Jesus is the Son of God, and this realization bursts out of him not on the basis of Jesus' miracles, or on the basis of signs or wonders, but on "how Jesus died." That is the thing that catches his attention. It is not the escape route that attracts the centurion but rather Jesus' willing endurance. The many characters around the cross put us in touch with many aspects of ourselves; they help us to identify with our critical side, enabling us to watch the scoffing and mockery we are capable of. They open for us our negative attitudes as we gaze on the two thieves; we confront ourselves in Pilate and the high priest, in Peter and the apostles, and in all of them we are found wanting. In the centurion alone do we find the doorway. His assertion about Christ springs from empathy and understanding. He moves from the position of judgment that his vocation might lead us to expect of him to a position of empathizing and resonating with Jesus. "To pass judgment in Jung's sense is to place oneself in the superior position; to agree off-handedly is to place oneself in an attitude of inferiority. The personality

can cease to exist in two ways—either by destroying the other, or by being absorbed by the other—and maturity in interpersonal relationships demands that neither oneself nor the other shall disappear, but that each shall contribute to the affirmation and realization of the other's personality.[11] The centurion in me can enter into all the other partial aspects of my life and yet not lose sight of the goodness that is central to who I am. It is that aspect of me that is ever moving from judgment to empathy and, in the process, believing.

Chapter 19
Passion

Finally in our consideration of the passion we turn to consider its central character, Jesus. Mark stresses the deepening darkness of the passion. We see here the agonizing of Jesus, his isolation, his silence, and the mocking and taunting he was subjected to by the people around him. In the midst of this, as indeed throughout the Gospel, we see the life of extraordinary authenticity and originality that he manifested. In spite of the total falling apart of everything, in spite of the abandonments that he endured, in spite of the sufferings he underwent, he did not despair. He went into the tomb trusting that God would accept him as he was.

The passion is marked by a sense of donation, a sense of gift. Jesus is a gift of many people to many people. He is "handed over" by Judas to the Sanhedrin (14:10); he is "handed over" by the Sanhedrin to Pilate (15:1–10); he is "handed over" by Pilate to the soldiers (15:15); he is handed over by the soldiers to death (15:23); and in death, he is handed over by God to his own fate and destiny (15:34). This constantly being "handed over" and "delivered up" has about it a sense of betrayal but also there is an element of gift in it. Jesus' own handing over of his life is definitely gift. His whole life was a giving, a being for others, and he dies as he lived, overcoming and transcending the conflicts that were present, reconciling and healing them in himself.

Gradually he becomes more and more isolated. Having already lost the support of the crowds, now he will go through the gradual loss of everyone else. First the larger crowd of apostles leave, then the twelve, then the great ones, Peter, James, and John, and finally he is abandoned by the Father. His isolation begins with the falling asleep of the disciples in Gethsemani, advances through the kiss of Judas, is highlighted in the trial before the Sanhedrin, crests through the denials of Peter, and is climaxed in the cry from the cross which goes unanswered by the Father. As the isolation grows the silence deepens. The silence is more pronounced in the passion especially when we compare it with the passion narratives in the other Gospels. The isolation is heightened by the situation that exists around him. He is crucified between two thieves, royally enthroned in mockery, judged by false witnesses, surrounded by derision, and abandoned by all.

Silence can mean many things. We have all witnessed different types of it, from the cautious silence to the angry silence, from the pregnant silence to the loving silence. What then is this kind of silence that is evidenced in the passion? Two things seem to emerge that are consistent with his stance throughout the Gospel as a whole. Here he refuses a certain type of Messiahship; he also refuses a certain kind of suffering. He avoids both tyranny and slavery, both sadism and masochism. To say he enjoyed suffering would be contrary to his cry in Gethsemani and on the cross. It would portray a terrible caricature of the God he proclaimed.

Mark emphasizes the silence in a number of ways. He has Jesus speak on very few occasions during the passion. Whenever he does speak he has him give short brief replies. Mark draws direct attention to the silence on a number of occasions, e.g., "Jesus kept quiet and would not say a word" (14:61), and again "Jesus refused to say a word and Pilate was filled with surprise" (15:5). Throughout the Gospel the command to silence is closely connected with the question of identity. The question that keeps creeping back into the silences and conflict of the passion is the same. Who is this?

Pilate the secular leader puts it like this: "Are you the King of the Jews?" Jesus answers: "So you say." The high priest, the religious leader, puts it like this: "Are you the Messiah, the Son of the Blessed God?" Jesus answers: "I am. And you will see the Son of Man seated at the right side of the Almighty and coming with the clouds of heaven."

Both the secular and religious worlds are questioning, or, better still, inquesting, the identity of Jesus, and they do so in terms of his roles, his persona. He responds by affirming himself in both of the roles they offer him. Nevertheless he does not accept either role as the ultimate definition, or synopsis, or statement, about himself. In fact he elaborates their question into a bigger one. He turns back to God with the identity question on his own lips:

God — Silent
Jesus— Eloi, Eloi lama sabachthani. My God, my God, why have you abandoned me?
God — Silent.

This is extremely important. Jesus reaches into his own life where he himself is a question addressed to his own existence, to the cosmos, to the ultimate, and the ultimate remains silent. Jesus enters the moment of his death with the question of his ultimate identity still before the reader, the disciple, the follower. The silence of Jesus at this point meets and encounters the silence of God.

Meister Eckhart,[1] the fourteenth century German mystic, is a great help here to our understanding. He holds a dipolar doctrine of God in which he distinguishes between the manifesting aspect of God, which he calls the Trinity, and the non-manifesting aspect of God, which he calls the Godhead. This aspect of God he calls the abyss of the divinity or the darkness of God. Here God is incomprehensible, he is the unnatured natured, and here there is no activity. This is in contrast to the Trinity, which is the dynamic side of God, that he refers to occasionally as the bubbling water or the spouting fire. Eckhart says that the soul must enter the desert of the Godhead which he calls the sepulchre of the soul, where the ego is annihilated. This darkness of God is the final mystery, or, as Eckhart himself puts it:

> The Father is the beginning of the Godhead because he understands himself in himself. It is from the Father that the eternal word, though always remaining within, nevertheless goes out, and the Father does not give birth to him, for he remains within and is the goal of the Godhead and all creatures, the one in whom there is pure peace and rest for everything which ever received being. The beginning is for the sake of the final goal, for in that final end everything rests which ever received existence endowed with reason. The final goal of being is the darkness or the unknowability of the hidden divinity, which is that light that shines but the darkness has not comprehended it.[2]

It is into this darkness that Jesus goes with the question that he is, trusting nothing other than the Father. He enters

this abyss and darkness. He goes beyond roles and defini-
tions, even beyond naming himself. He goes into his own
silence where he is ultimately a question. He enters with his
own silence and darkness into the silent darkness of the
Father. This is what the vulnerability of Christ is, insofar as
I can see and understand it. The vulnerability of the passion
is much greater than the vulnerability exhibited in terms of
his relationship to his disciples and his opponents. The terrible pain and agony of the passion is truly reflected in his
physical and emotional suffering. It is truly heightened by
the aloneness that comes to him when his supporters flee.
Nevertheless the deeper pain only emerges at this point in
its full force. Jesus knows what will happen vis-à-vis the
opponents. He knows what will happen to the disciples.
What remains, and what he has to trust at this moment, is
what happens vis-à-vis the Father. It is in this, and precisely
in this, that the Gospel comes as good news to us. It is in
this that it comes as a proclamation of healing and possibility in the midst of lostness.

Sebastian Moore asks the questions "How is Christ's
death salvific?" and "What is the motivation for the killing
of Jesus?"[3] He finds clues to the answer in the feeling that
we have failed either another person or the mysterious otherness in which we live. This feeling he describes as fear.

Beyond it there is a sense of guilt that tends to swallow
us up. This sense of guilt isolates us and leaves us desolate,
and in this condition God is no more. Anything that lifts
this depression, guilt, isolation, desolation, absence of God,
can, he says, only be the touch of God. Jesus entered this
condition and took it with him into death. This sense,
which I believe is the silence of ultimate identity, is what
Jesus brings into the silence of God. This is the passion that
is not a moment but a lifetime. Jesus hurls this question
from the cross into the silence of an apparently indifferent

God and so takes with him to death the ultimate question of every person. Thomas Merton[4] in a similar fashion says that man chose initially to commit his freedom to an illusion and so placed himself in darkness. He always remained however as one who desired the light, longed for order and peace. In his "non-entity he could not help but aspire to being, to spiritual liberty, to true identity."

Jesus takes with him into death the suspicion (Moore calls it guilt) that because I am nothing I am somehow a failure, I am lost, I am worthless. He takes with him the hope (Moore's desire to be the beloved of the beloved; Merton's aspiration for being) to be someone. He takes this hope together with the suspicion that I am no one. He takes therefore the circle of depression (Moore calls it desolation) and he carries all of this right into the silence of God that Eckhart calls the Godhead. He takes all of this into that darkness, and there he makes his discovery. Sam Keen makes the observation that "our true identity lies on the other side of fear" and that the "fear of going too far keeps us from going far enough."[5] Jesus was not afraid to go too far. He entered through death into the darkness of the Godhead.

The passion story is carefully arranged and presented by Mark. The trial is designed to show the culpability and guilt of Christ. It fails, and the truth emerges—namely, there are no facts to support the accusation. The accusation however does not go away. The cloud of suspicion remains. The trial, designed to show his guilt, concludes by proclaiming his dignity but no one accepts it. Everyone—the priests, leaders, apostles, etc.—leaves and deserts him. The proclamation is met instead with blasphemy, condemnation, denial and silence. Jesus is now alone. What he does at this juncture is what we fail to do. He faces into his death and takes with him the suspicion, the guilt, the fear, and the desire, and in death he awaits the response to that desire, to that question that he is. How delightful then that Mark has the centurion, the experienced alien, the symbolic darkness of Rome, utter the closing truth (15:39). The darkness speaks the true identity.

God has always been incomprehensible as Eckhart pointed out. Scripture clearly states, "My ways are not your ways" (Is 55:8). God is beyond our understanding. Rahner speaks of our need to let ourselves fall into the "incomprehensibility of God as into our true fulfillment and happiness."[6] This is what Jesus is doing in the Markan passion. He falls forward, or, better still, he moves forward, he surrenders to the darkness of God, a darkness that he trusts. Teilhard prayerfully speaks of this moment in his own life as it draws to a close and he asks his God that death be a communion with him:

> When the signs of age begin to mark my body (and still more when they touch my mind); when the ill that is to diminish me or carry me off strikes from without or is born within me; when the painful moment comes in which I suddenly awaken to the fact that I am ill or growing old; and above all at that last moment when I feel I am losing hold of myself and am absolutely passive within the hands of the great unknown forces that have formed me; in all those dark moments, O God, grant that I may understand that it is you (provided only my faith is strong enough) who are painfully parting the fibers of my being in order to penetrate to the very marrow of my substance and bear me away within yourself. The more deeply and incurably the evil is encrusted in my flesh the more it will be you that I am harboring . . . you as a loving active principle of puri-

fication and detachment. The more the future opens
before me like some dizzy abyss or dark tunnel, the
more confident I may be . . . if I venture forward on the
strength of your word, of losing myself and surrendering myself in you, of being assimilated by your body
Jesus.

You are the irresistible and vivifying force, O Lord, and
because yours is the energy, because, of the two of us,
you are infinitely the stronger, it is on you that falls the
part of consuming me in the union that should weld us
together. Vouchsafe, therefore, something more precious still than the grace for which all the faithful pray.
It is not enough that I should die while communicating.
Teach me to treat my death as an act of communion.[7]

Chapter 20
Beyond an Empty Tomb

Mark brings his Gospel to a close with the story of the empty tomb in 16:1–8. To this story, at a later period in history, is added a second ending (16:9–20), sometimes called the appendix or longer ending. This second ending mentions some appearances of Jesus to his followers as the risen one. Together they form the basis for our closing reflections.

Initially the story is a story about women coming to the tomb to anoint Jesus after his death. The story, as it begins and develops, is a story about closure and about death. The tone of the story is heavy and somewhat depressing. The emphasis in the story reflects the mindset of the women immediately following the burial. They are concerned about the large stone that sealed the tomb. They expect to find a corpse. They intend to anoint the body. They obviously are geared to meet death as the absolute which claimed the life of Jesus, and they were present to bring closure to that life. Schillebeeckx observes that "a biblical anthropology establishes a close relation between the status of women and death."[1] They were given the tasks of weeping, mourning, preparing the body, visiting the graves, etc.

These women then wish to grieve as mourners and to honor their dead friend. They are certainly not expecting anything like the events they encounter.

Once they reach the grave, conversation ceases. The story leads us to understand that all their expectations are reversed by the events that now take place. Their world is turned upside down and inside out. They look for a tomb filled with a corpse. They find it emptied of death. They expect a stone to seal it, they find it rolled away. They expect no word from the tomb but they receive a clear message. They expect to stay some time at the grave. They are ordered back to Galilee immediately. They expect to mourn for a while but their thoughts are clearly directed away from their consuming preoccupation with death to the life that lies ahead of them in Galilee.

When they enter the tomb they meet a young man in a white robe seated at the right hand side, a fact that Benoit[2] notes is associated with the nobler side. Who is this young man? It is clear that here he functions as a messenger, and while Mark refers to him as a young man, Matthew refers to the presence of an angel. It is not uncommon for angels to appear in biblical stories as messengers and interpreters of the will of God, or bearers of his command. Generally when this occurs their appearance triggers both fear and amazement in the people they visit. Both of these reactions are found in the story. This messenger, or angel, or young man reduces the fear of the women, draws their attention to the emptiness of the tomb and redirects their energy so that they may be witnesses to others of Jesus as living and present among them.

An empty tomb, however, is of itself only an empty tomb. Schillebeeckx observes that "nowhere is there any inference from an empty tomb to the resurrection . . . the other way round in fact. 'He is risen . . . he is not here.'"[3]

How does this come about? The custom of visiting the graves was common in and around Jerusalem. It was the practice of people to visit the tomb of Jesus. On such an occasion the pilgrims would probably hear a sermon or would share together their faith in the resurrection. In this story then the angel announces that faith of the community and this faith is that Jesus has gone forward into a new type of existence. He is no longer here in this empty place. This leads Schillebeeckx to assert that "the resurrection, Mark 16:1–8, is a mystery of faith, of which this holy place is the negative symbol."[4]

What is this new form of existence to which Jesus has gone forward? In this second ending, which we have alluded to earlier, Mark gives some hints. These hints can be further elaborated on through a comparison with the resurrection stories in the other Gospels. Mark, as the story reads, moves us from the empty tomb to the risen Christ. He portrays the risen Jesus as appearing to various people—first to Mary Magdalene, later on to two disciples out for a walk, and finally to a group seated at table. This triple assertion maintains the by now familiar Markan technique for emphasizing an event, and here it draws attention to the resurrection, to the new life of Jesus. Clearly the implication is that this new life is different. The other Gospel accounts of the resurrection are a help to us in filling out something of that difference. There is much confusion in the stories. Did Jesus appear first in Jerusalem or in Galilee? Was it on Easter Sunday night or during the week that he first appeared? Was it a man or two men, an angel or two angels, who met the disciples and the women at the grave? The details are at times contradictory. Nevertheless all the stories show that Jesus' existence is now different from the existence he had prior to his death. At times he is unrecognizable, as when he meets Mary Magdalene in John

20:14, or when Peter sees him in John 21, or when he meets the men on the road to Emmaus in Luke 24. On other occasions he is clearly recognizable. At times he vanishes from one place to show up nearly immediately somewhere else as in Luke 24:31 and 24:36. He has a capacity to enter through locked doors at will, as in John 20:26. And he doesn't seem to be concerned any longer about obstacles, whether they are external objects or internal fears. He is a Jesus beyond human limits and restrictions. Raymond Brown says that the Gospel accounts "hint at the radically changed status of the one who appears . . . [He has been] transferred into the realm of Lordship, which is the realm of God.[5]

Mark in the appendix to his Gospel summarizes the appearances of Jesus in vv. 9–15. This was probably done for catechetical purposes later in history. The summary statement, however, is consistent with the points we made above about the changed manner of Jesus' existence. Mark then proceeds to the command of Jesus to his disciples regarding mission. Each of the Gospel accounts stresses this responsibility that is given to the disciples. Mark's particular emphasis stresses both the value and possibility of freedom as well as the reality and possibility of bondage and condemnation envisaged by the mission. Those who believe and are baptized will be saved; those who do not believe will be condemned.

Mark finally notes that there will be signs that will be associated with believers; they will cast out devils, they will have the gift of tongues, they will pick up snakes in their hands, they will be unharmed if they drink poison, they will lay their hands on the sick who will recover (16:17–18).

Entering these stories as a story of the self I begin to be aware of a new urging arising within me. The thought of Chardin comes back to my mind to shed light on the story.

Teilhard[6] noted that "true union does not fuse the elements
it brings together but gives them a renewal of vitality." It is,
he maintained, "egoism that hardens and neutralizes the
human stuff. Union differentiates." And so he says that it is
by coinciding with all the rest that we shall find the center
of ourselves. This is the mission that the apostles are
charged with following the resurrection. We are called out
to be what Paul calls the body of Christ, what theologians
call the Church, what Teilhard calls the "phylum of love."
Death is an entry, a barrier, an obstacle, a passageway to a
new mode of existence, and so ahead of man there is a genuine super-love, an attracting super-person, a focus of con-
vergence for the whole universe. Gradually the self leads
me beyond my own limited tomb out to Galilee, out to
unite with a whole cosmos in transition and in journey.

Mark however envisages the possibility of condemnation. It is possible to turn back or away from this mission
and summons to a smaller and at times more secure looking
world. John Sanford,[7] commenting on the writings of Fritz
Kunkel and Carl Jung, makes the observation that on one
important point they seem to differ. Jung does not have the
concept of egocentricity while Kunkel does. Jung talks of a
one-sided development of the ego which leads to its collapse. Kunkel points out that this one-sided development is
in the service of the ego's egocentricity. Because Jung does
not have Kunkel's concept of egocentricity he is forced to
project evil into the self and also into God. Kunkel on the
other hand avoids this difficulty. The ego can center on
itself and become absorbed with its own limited existence
while ignoring the deeper self. This is to embrace what I
believe Mark calls condemnation. One lives a very jaun-
diced existence locked into a tomb from which there can be
no escape apart from love.

I come then to this Markan story, realizing that I have a choice before me either to turn back into "condemnation" and a limited ego existence or to move forward, joining with other centers in a phylum of love, advancing toward the personalizing center of the universe. Either the whole universe is moving forward by choice or we are intensely isolating in an existence of disorder, violence and destructive competition. In prayer I begin to identify the compassionate side of my own life that comes to mourn and grieve the death of my own ego. I permit this attitude of compassion and care to lead me to the dead areas of my life, to the empty tombs, and the well sealed but threatened powers of my own ego, self-esteem and importance. As I begin to arrive at this place, this space within me to preside over this death, a new voice is heard. I discover an indicator, a pointer, a messenger in the activity of my mind and will. It directs my attention outward again to a larger world. It says Jesus is risen. He is not here; you will find him in Galilee. He is not here in this place. I am called out to other centers of love, and as I turn toward them I find great gifts between us to heal, to affirm, to enliven. It is here that I now begin to discover increasing freedom, awareness, relatedness and transcendence.

Notes

Preface

1. T. S. Eliot, *Four Quarters*, Harcourt Brace Jovanovich: New York, 1943.
2. John D. Carter and Bruce Narramore, *The Integration of Psychology and Theology*, Rosemead Psychology Series, Zondervan: Grand Rapids, 1979, p. 71.
3. For a further discussion of this matter the following can be recommended: John D. Carter, "Secular and Sacred Models of Psychology and Religion," *Journal of Psychology and Theology* 5, Summer, 1977, pp. 197–208; Howard Clinebell, Jr., *The Mental Health Ministry Of The Local Church*, Abingdon Press: New York, 1965; Wallace B. Clift, *Jung and Christianity: The Challenge of Reconciliation*, Crossroad: New York, 1983; Victor White, *God and the Unconscious*, Meridian Books, World Publishing Co.: New York, 1961; Gary Collins, *Psychology and Theology Prospects for Integration*, ed. H. Nowton Malony, Abington: Nashville, 1981; Paul C. Vitz, *Psychology as Religion: The Cult of Self Worship*, Eerdmans: Grand Rapids, 1977.

Chapter 1—Beginning

1. Sean P. Kealy, C. S. Sp., *Mark's Gospel: A History of Its Interpretation*, Paulist Press: New York, 1982. In the seven major

192

sections of this work Kealy covers studies of the Markan Gospel as follows: a. First Five Centuries: b. Decline of Mark: Middle Ages to the Eighteenth Century; c. Mark the First Gospel: Reimerus and the Nineteenth Century Liberals; d. Mark the Theologian: Wrede and the Twentieth Century; e. Form Critics; f. Marsen and the Redaction Critics; g. Mark Restored: 1969 Onward.

2. Werner Kelber, *The Kingdom in Mark: A New Place and a New Time,* Fortress Press: Philadelphia, 1974; *Mark's Story of Jesus,* Fortress Press: Philadelphia, 1979; *Passion in Mark,* Fortress Press: Philadelphia, 1976.

3. Donald Michie and David Rhoads, *Mark as Story,* Fortress Press: Philadelphia, 1982.

4. Werner Kelber, *Mark's Story of Jesus, op. cit.,* p. 11.

5. Donald Michie and David Rhoads, *Mark as Story, op. cit.,* p. 3.

6. Carl Gustav Jung, *Collected Works,* trans. R. F. C. Hull, Bollingen Series, published in twenty volumes by Princeton University Press.

7. Carl Gustav Jung, *Collected Works,* "The Structure and Dynamics of the Psyche," *op cit.,* Vol. 8; "The Archetypes and the Collective Unconsicous," *op cit.,* Vol. 9; "Two Essays on Analytical Psychology," *op. cit.,* vol. 7.

8. Susan Muto, *Practical Guide to Spiritual Reading,* Dimension Books: Denville, 1976, pp. 1–41.

Chapter 2—Good News

1. Edward Schillebeeckx, *Jesus,* Seabury Press: New York, 1979, pp. 109f.

2. Werner Kelber, *Mark's Story of Jesus,* Fortress Press: Philadelphia, 1979, p. 18.

3. T. S. Eliot, *The Four Quartets,* "Little Gidding," Harcourt Brace Jovanovich: New York, 1943.

4. Werner Kelber, *Mark's Story of Jesus,* Fortress Press: Philadelphia, 1979, p. 17.

5. John S. Dunne, *A Search for God in Time and Memory,* Collier Macmillan, Ltd.: London, 1970.

6. *Ibid.,* p. 9.

7. Cf. J. E. Cirlot, *A Dictionary of Symbols*, Philosophical Library: New York, 1982, p. 233.
8. Edward Edinger, *Ego and Archetype*, Penguin Books: Maryland, 1972, p. 137.

Chapter 3—The Desert

1. D. E. Nineham, *Saint Mark*, Penguin Books: Baltimore, 1963, pp. 63–64.
2. Percy B. Shelley, *Ozymandias of Egypt*, as reprinted in *Standard Book of British and American Verse*, Doubleday: Garden City, 1932, p. 359.
3. Alan W. Jones, *Journey into Christ*, Seabury Press: New York, 1977, p. 17.
4. Evelyn Whitehead and James D. Whitehead, *Christian Life Patterns*, Doubleday: Garden City, 1979, pp. 27–28.
5. Michael Novak, *Ascent of the Mountain, Flight of the Dove*, Harper and Row: New York, 1971, pp. 85–86. Cf. also *The Experience of Nothingness*, Harper Books: New York, 1970. In both of these works Novak examines the experience of nothingness not only in its personal dimension but also in its interpersonal and societal dimensions. He shows how the impact of one's culture, world, society, etc., impacts on one's sense of reality and one's sense of identity. His exploration of the topic is one that I return to again later in this book.
6. Merritt Molloy, "Mohawk Ridge," in *My Song for Him Who Never Sang for Me*, Ward Ritchie Press, 1975, p. 139.
7. Alan W. Jones, *Journey into Christ, op cit.*, p. 57.

Chapter 4—The Call

1. Raymond Brown, ed., *Peter in the New Testament*, Augsburg: Minneapolis, 1973, pp. 60f.
2. Theodore Weeden, *Traditions in Conflict*, Fortress Press: Philadelphia, 1971, pp. 26–51.
3. Edward Schillebeeckx, *Jesus, op. cit.*, pp. 220–229.
4. Theodore Weeden, *Traditions in Conflict, op. cit.*

5. Carl Gustav Jung, *Collected Works, op cit.*, Vol. 6.

6. *Ibid.*

7. Thomas S. Kane, *Journey of the Heart*, St. Bede's Publications: Still River, Massachusetts, 1979.

8. There is extensive discussion on the disciples in the Markan Gospel. We can refer to just a few publications: David Rhoads and Donald Michie, *Mark as Story*, Fortress Press: Philadelphia, 1982; Robert Tannehill, "The Disciples in Mark: The Function of a Narrative Role," *Journal of Religion* 57, 1977; Werner Kelber, *Mark's Story of Jesus*, Fortress Press: Philadelphia, 1979; Theodore Weeden, *Traditions in Conflict*, Fortress Press: Philadelphia, 1971; Joanna Dewey, *Disciples of the Way: Mark on Discipleship*, Board of Global Ministries, United Methodist Church, 1976.

9. Chirstopher Grannis, Arthur Laffin, Erin Schade, *The Risk of the Cross: Christian Discipleship in the Nuclear Age*, Seabury Press: New York, 1981, p. 4.

Chapter 5—A Typical Day

1. Wilfred Harrington, O. P., *Mark, New Testament Message*, Vol. 4, Michael Glazier: Wilmington, 1979, p. 15.

2. D. E. Nineham, *Saint Mark, op. cit.*, p. 74.

3. Gunther Bornkam, *Jesus of Nazareth*, Harper and Row: New York, 1975, p. 96.

4. Rudolph Schnackenburg, *The Gospel According to Saint Mark*, Vol. 1, p. 30 in *New Testament for Spiritual Reading*, John L. McKenzie, ed., Herder and Herder: New York, 1971.

5. R. H. Lightfoot, *The Gospel of St. Mark*, Oxford University Press: London, 1962.

6. James Hillman, *Insearch—Psychology and Religion*, Charles Scribner and Sons: New York, 1967.

7. Eduard Schweizer, *The Good News According to Mark*, John Knox Press: Atlanta, 1977, p. 53.

8. Edward C. Whitmont, *The Symbolic Quest*, Princeton University Press: New Jersey, 1978, p. 185.

9. Anne Marie Gallagher, R. S. M., "The Negotiation of the Contrasexual Opposites Animus and Anima and Its Implication for the Pastoral Man and Woman," in *Journal of Pastoral Counseling,* Robert A. Burns, ed., Vol XIV, No. 1, Spring-Summer, 1979, Iona College: New York, 1979, p. 59.

10. M. L. Von Franz, "Process of Individuation," in C. G. Jung, *Man and His Symbols,* Doubleday: New York, 1979, p. 177. Cf. also Whitmont: "As a numinous image, namely as an affective image spontaneously produced by the objective psyche, the anima represents the eternal feminine—in any and all of her four possible aspects and their variants and combinations as Mother, Hetaira, Amazon and Medium. She appears as the goddess of nature, Dea Natura, and the great goddess of Moon and Earth who is mother, sister, beloved, destroyer, beautiful enchantress, ugly witch, life and death all in one person or in various aspects of the one; thus she appears in innumerable images of enchanting, frightening, friendly, helpful, or dangerous feminine figures, or even in animal figures as we have seen—foremost as cat, snake, horse, cow, dove, owl, which mythology assigns to certain feminine deities. She appears as seductress, harlot, nymph, muse, saint, martyr, maiden in distress, gypsy, peasant woman, the lady next door, or as the Queen of Heaven, the Holy Virgin, to mention but a few examples": Edward C. Whitmont, *The Symbolic Quest, op cit.,* p. 189.

11. Catherine O'Connor, *Woman and Cosmos: The Feminine in the Thought of Pierre de Chardin,* Prentice-Hall: New Jersey, 1971.

12. Dante Aligheri, *The Divine Comedy,* trans. by D. Sayers and B. Reynolds: I. Inferno, Penguin: Baltimore, 1949; II. Purgatorio, Penguin: Baltimore, 1955; III. Paradiso, Penguin: Baltimore, 1962.

13. Eduard Schweizer, *The Good News According to Mark, op cit.,* p. 56.

14. Wilfred Harrington, *Mark, New Testament Message, op cit.,* p. 20.

15. Viktor E. Frankl, *Psychotherapy and Existentialism: Selected Papers on Logotherapy,* Simon and Schuster: New York, 1967, p. 10.

16. "Turning and turning in the widening gyre
The falcon cannot hear the falconer
Things fall apart; the center cannot hold
Mere anarchy is loosed upon the world
The blood dimmed tide is loosed and everywhere
The ceremony of innocence is drowned
The best lack all conviction while the worst
Are full of Passionate intensity."

William Butler Yeats, "The Second Coming," in Jacob Trapp, ed., *Modern Religious Poems*, Harper and Row: New York, 1964, p. 236.
17. Henri Nouwen, *Reaching Out: The Three Movements of the Spiritual Life*, Doubleday: Garden City, 1966.
18. Werner Kelber, *Mark's Story of Jesus, op cit.*, p. 22.
19. Wilfred Harrington, *Mark, New Testament Message, op cit.*, p. 21.

Chapter 6—Conflict

1. David Rhoads and Donald Michie, *Mark as Story, op. cit.*, pp. 73f.
2. *Ibid.*, p. 86.
3. *Ibid.*, particularly "Episodes In Concentric Patterns," pp. 51–54.
4. Sam Keen, *To a Dancing God*, Harper and Row: New York, 1970, p. 28.
5. David Rhoads and Donald Michie, *Mark as Story, op. cit.*, p. 129.
6. D. E. Nineham, *Saint Mark, op cit.*, p. 99.
7. Eduard Schweizer, *The Good News According to Mark, op cit.*, p. 66.
8. Robert Assagoli, *Psychosynthesis*, Penguin Books: New York 1977, p. 22.
9. Virginia Satir, *Peoplemaking*, Science and Behaviour Books, Inc.: Palo Alto, 1972, p. 66.
10. Carl Gustav Jung, *Collected Works*, Volume 9, Part II, Aion.

11. Teilhard de Chardin, *Making of a Mind,* Harper and Row: New York, 1965. I have rearranged the prose wording so as to highlight the different aspect of hands suggested in the meditation. Another excellent meditation along similar lines is suggested in Edward Farrell's *Surprised by the Spirit.*
12. Mary A. Schaldenbrand, "Time, the Self and Hope" in *The Future as the Presence of Shared Hope,* Maryellen Muckenhirn, ed., Sheed and Ward: New York, 1968, p. 116.
13. Carl Gustav Jung, *Collected Works,* "Two Essays on Analytical Psychology," Volume 7, par. 78.

Chapter 7—The Crossing

1. Werner Kelber, *Mark's Story of Jesus, op. cit.,* pp. 30f.
2. *Ibid.*
3. St. Bonaventure, *The Soul's Journey into God,* Classics of Western Spirituality, Paulist Press: New York, 1978, *idem, The Mind's Road to God,* Bobbs Merrill Co.: Indianapolis, 1975; Ewert Cousins, *Bonaventure and the Coincidence of Opposites,* Franciscan Herald Press: Chicago, 1979.
4. Edward Edinger, *Ego and Archetype, op. cit.,* p. 40.
5. Erich Neumann, "On the Moon and Martiarchal Consciousness," as quoted by Edward Edinger in *Ego and Archetype, op. cit.,* p. 279.
6. Wilfred Harrington, *Mark, op cit.,* p. 64.
7. T. S. Eliot, *Four Quartets,* Harcourt, Brace and World: New York, 1943. The theme of the still point moves throughout the *Four Quartets.* It is a point that defies definition. Nevertheless it is a point that can be understood through paradox. It is a point which controls all movement even though it is a point where there is no movement. Eliot puts it this way in "Burnt Norton" (p. 15):

"At the still point of the turning world. Neither flesh nor fleshless:
Neither from nor towards; at the still point, there the dance is,

But neither arrest nor movement. And do not call it fixity,
Where past and future are gathered. Neither movement from
    nor towards,
Neither accent nor decline. Except for the point, the still point,
There would be no dance, and there is only the dance.

8. In "East Coker," *Four Quartets*, Eliot says (p. 26):

. . . We are only undeceived
Of that which, deceiving, could no longer harm.
In the middle, not only in the middle of the way
But all the way, in a dark wood, in a bramble,
On the edge of a grimpen, where is no secure foothold,
And menaced by monsters, fancy lights.
Risking enchantment.

9. Elliot sees now that where there is no faith in a purpose there
can be no prayer. Life then is just moving along, a drifting.
His lines describe this kind of existence in which life is without value and meaning. It is into this that he places by contrast with its emptiness all the powerful emotion of the following lines from "Dry Salvages" (*Four Quartets*, p. 57).

There is no end, but addition: the trailing
Consequence of further days and hours,
While emotion takes to itself the emotionless
Years of living among the breakage
Of what was believed in as the most reliable—
And therefore the fittest for renunciation.

There is the final addition, the failing
Pride or resentment at failing powers,
The unattached devotion which might pass for devotionless,
In a drifting boat with a slow leakage,
The silent listening to the undeniable
Clamour of the bell of the last annunciation.

10. T. S. Eliot, "Journey of the Magi," in *Selected Poems*, Harcourt Brace and World: New York, 1964, p. 98.

Chapter 8—The Shadow

1. Jolande Jacobi, *The Way of Individuation*, Harcourt, Brace and World: New York, 1967, p. 61.
2. *Ibid.*
3. Erich Neumann, *Depth Psychology and a New Ethic*, Harper and Row: New York, 1973, p. 50.
4. *Ibid.*, p. 38.
5. Werner Kelber, *Mark's Story of Jesus*, op. cit., p. 151.
6. Gerasa is thirty-three miles southeast of Lake Gennesaret and therefore an unsuitable locale in view of 5:13. Variant readings are Gadarenes (of Gadara six miles south east of the lake) and Gergesenes (of Gergesa, an otherwise unidentified place). At all events Jesus is in pagan territory and his presence there reflects Isaiah 65:1. Raymond Brown, Joseph Fitzmyer, Roland E. Murphy, eds., *Jerome Biblical Commentary*, Prentice-Hall: Englewood Cliffs, 1968, Vol. 2, p. 33.
7. D. E. Nineham, *Saint Mark*, op. cit., p. 151.
8. Eduard Schweizer, *The Good News According to Mark*, op cit., p. 114.
9. Joseph Campbell, *The Masks of God: Primitive Mythology*, Penguin, 1975, p. 120–200; *Occidental Mythology*, Penguin, 1977, p. 154 and pp. 171–176; *Creative Mythology*, Penguin, 1976, pp. 124–128 and pp. 205–207.
10. Arthur Vogel, *Body Theology*, Harper and Row: New York, 1973, p. 88.
11. Norman Cameron, *Personality Development and Psychopathology*, Houghton Mifflin: Boston, 1963, pp. 679f.
12. Carl E. and LaVonne Braaten, *The Living Temple*, Harper and Row: New York, 1976, pp. 26–27.
13. Erich Neumann, *Depth Psychology and a New Ethic*, op. cit., p. 95.

Chapter 9—The Feminine

1. Mk 2:30. There is also a reference to his mother in 3:31.
2. Werner Kelber, *Mark's Story of Jesus, op cit.*, p. 38.
3. Marie Louis Von Franz, "The Process of Individuation," in *Man and His Symbols*, C. G. Jung, ed., Doubleday: New York, 1979, p. 177.
4. "The picture of woman obtained from the Old Testament laws can be summarized in the first instance as that of a legal non-person; where she does become visible it is as a dependent and usually an inferior, in a male centered and male dominated society. The laws by and large do not address her; most do not even acknowledge her existence. She comes to view only in situations a. where males are lacking in essential socio-economic roles (the female heir), b. where she requires special protection (the widow), c. where sexual offenses involving women are treated, and d. where sexually defined or sexually differentiated states, roles and/or occupations are dealt with (the female slave or captive as wife, the woman as mother, and the sorceress): where ranking occurs she is always inferior to the male. Only in her role as mother is she accorded status and honor equivalent to a man's. Nevertheless she is always subject to the authority of some male (father, husband, or brother), except when widowed or divorced—an existentially precarious type of independence in Israel": Phyllis Bird, "Images of Women in the Old Testament," in Rosemary Radford Ruether, ed., *Religion and Sexism: Images of Women in the Jewish and Christian Traditions*, Simon and Schuster: New York, 1974, pp. 56–57.
5. Hans Walter Wolf, *Anthropology of the Old Testament*, Fortress Press: Philadelphia, 1974, p. 61.
6. Werner Kelber, *Mark's Story of Jesus, op cit.*, p. 32.
7. Alicia Faxon, *Woman and Jesus*, United Church Press: Philadelphia, 1973, pp. 57–58.
8. Marie Louis Van Franz, "The Process of Individuation," in C. G. Jung, *Man and His Symbols, op. cit.*, p. 179.
9. *Ibid.* p. 186.

10. "For the sake of individuation it is necessary for (one) to find out what this other (partial) personality is like, how it feels, thinks and tends to act. In a given situation one has to consider not only one's own reaction but also how the anima (animus) reacts, what she desires, likes or dislikes. Like a problematical partner the anima (animus) has to be treated with attention and consideration but also with discipline and experimental interplay and challenge": Edward C. Whitmont, *The Symbolic Quest, op. cit.*, p. 85.

11. Alicia Faxon, *Woman and Jesus, op. cit.*, p. 50.

12. Jean Gill, *Images of My Self*, Paulist Press: New York, 1982, p. 35.

13. *Ibid.*, p. 38.

14. James Hillman *Insearch—Psychology and Religion*, Charles Scribner and Sons: New York, 1967, p. 101, as quoted in John Welch O. Carm., *Spiritual Pilgrims: Carl Jung and Teresa of Avila*, Paulist Press: New York, 1982, p. 174.

15. "Like the anima the animus appears in a great variety of images, in fantasies or dreams, or projected in making fantasy upon a man. It takes the shape of any variation or combination of the four types of masculinity . . . Father, Puer (Son), Hero or Wise Man. The Father variations are authority figures of all sorts, ranging from the actual personal father or grandfather, or just the "ideal husband" as pater familias. The Son or Puer Aeternus figure may appear as brother, son, friend, ideal lover and partner, the fellow next door, the unknown lover, gentleman, huntsman, seducer, or even bum, or any mythological or fairy tale figure . . . Adonis, Prince Charming . . . which incorporates this image. The Hero may be a soldier, knight, or even coachman, chauffeur, or powerful boxer, or wrestler, Achilles, Sir Lancelot, or President Kennedy, a plain brute, rapist, or destroyer, or simply the exciting or fascinating elevator man with the blue eyes. The Wise Man may appear as great teacher, guru, sage, magician, prophet, guardian of the treasure, or as one's high school teacher, or simply the Mr. X who claims to know, or as one's analyst is presumed to

know all the answers": Edward C. Whitmont, *The Symbolic Quest, op. cit.*, p. 207.

Chapter 10—The Loaf

1. Mk 6:34–44: 8:1–9: 8:13f. In fact in this section bread is a very powerful symbol mentioned no less than six times.
2. For further discussion of this matter cf. James Plasteras, *The God of Exodus*, Bruce: Milwaukee, 1966, pp. 226f.
3. Joseph Campbell, *The Masks of God: Primitive Mythology, op. cit.*, p. 200.
4. Karl Rahner, *Belief Today*, Sheed and Ward: New York, 1967, pp. 32–33.
5. Vernon Robbins points to this also when he speaks of the Last Supper and makes the following observation, "Jesus' explanation of the meaning of the bread and the cup contrasts with Mark 6 to 8 where the disciples never grasp the significance of Jesus' distribution of bread and fish to large crowds. Therefore the drama of the Last Supper, in which eating is linked with Jesus' death resurrection and absence, completes the drama of the feeding stories": Vernon Robbins, "Last Meal: Preparation, Betrayal and Absence," in Werner Kelber, ed., *The Passion in Mark*, Fortress Press: Philadelphia, 1976, p. 22.
6. Werner Kelber, *Mark's Story of Jesus, op. cit.*, p. 40.
7. David Rhoads and Donald Michie, *Mark as Story, op. cit.*, p. 55.
8. It is interesting to note that this section has seven questions addressed to the disciples in quick succession. The whole thrust of the questions can be readily seen to aim at their lack of understanding.

   1. Why do you suppose that it is because you have no bread?
   2. Do you still not see or comprehend?
   3. Are your minds completely blinded?
   4. Have you eyes but no sight?
   5. Have you ears but no hearing?

6. How many baskets did you gather?
7. Do you still not understand?

9. Rudolf Schnackenburg, "The Gospel According to St. Mark," Vol. I, *New Testament for Spiritual Reading*, John McKenzie, ed., Herder and Herder: New York, 1971, pp. 140–141.
10. For a further discussion of these numbers in Jewish numerology cf. Heinisch Heidt, *Theology of the Old Testament*, Liturgical Press: Collegeville, 1955, pp. 103, 135, 150, 156, 171, 332, 345.
11. I have in mind Erikson's definition of crisis here: "It may be a good thing that the word crisis no longer connotes impending castastrophe which at one time seemed to be an obstacle to the understanding of the term. It has not been accepted as designating a necessary turning point, a crucial moment, when development must move one way or the other, marshalling resources of growth, recovery and further differentiation": Erik Erikson, *Identity Youth and Crisis*, W. W. Norton: New York, 1968, p. 16.
12. Werner Kelber, *Mark's Story of Jesus, op. cit.*, p. 41.
13. Bernard Lonergan, *The Subject*, Marquette University Press: Milwaukee, 1968, p. 9.

Chapter 11—Blindness and Sight

1. Gordon W. Allport, *The Individual and His Religion: A Psychological Interpretation*, Macmillan: New York, 1950.
2. Carl Gustav Jung, *Modern Man in Search of a Soul*, Harcourt, Brace, and World: New York, 1933, p. 229.
3. Levinson refers to a mid-life transition as a "somewhere between early adulthood and middle adulthood that is approximately between the ages of forty and forty-five": Daniel J. Levinson, *The Seasons of a Man's Life*, Ballantine: New York, 1978. Van Kaam says that the middle years begin at approximately the age of thirty. He distinguishes between a functional phase of the spiritual life, and a second phase of

the mid years "which may fall approximately between forty-four and fifty-five. . . . It is marked by a more pronounced occurrence of the transcendent crisis which initiates new forms of spiritual life in the history of human development": Adrian Van Kaam, C.S.S.P., *The Transcendent Self: Formative Spirituality of the Middle, Early, and Later Years of Life*, Dimension Books: New Jersey, 1979. Gail Sheehy refers to this time as the "spiritual dilemma of having no answers": Gail Sheehy, *Passages: Predictable Crises of Adult Life*, E. P. Dutton: New York, 1977.

4. Anna Freud, *The Ego and the Mechanisms of Defense*, Hogarth Press: London, 1937.

5. Daniel Levinson, *The Seasons of a Man's Life*, op. cit., p. 192.

6. William James O'Brien, *Stories to the Dark: Explorations in Religious Imagination*, Paulist Press: New York, 1977, pp. 114–122.

7. *Ibid.*

8. George Montague, S. M., *Mark: Good News for Hard Times*, Servant Books: Ann Arbor, 1981, p. 125.

9. Michael Crosby, *Spirituality of the Beatitudes: Matthew's Challenge for First World Christians*, Orbis Books: Maryknoll, 1980, p. 161.

10. Richard Byrne, *Living the Contemplative Dimension of Everyday Life*, unpublished dissertation: Pittsburgh: Duquesne University, 1973 as quoted and referred to in Michael Crosby, *Spirituality of the Beatitudes, Matthew's Challenge for First World Christians*, op. cit., pp. 160f.

11. Karen Horney, M. D., *Our Inner Conflicts: A Constructive Theory of Neurosis*, W. W. Norton: New York, 1972, p. 97.

12. As quoted in Violet S. de Laszlo, *Psyche and Symbol*, Doubleday: New York, 1958, pp. 113–132.

13. As quoted by James R. Zullo, *Mid Life: Crisis of Limits*, N. C. R. Cassettes: Kansas City, 1977. This is a quotation taken from the tapes, a series of four, by Dr. Zullo on the mid-life crisis.

14. Daniel Levinson, *The Seasons of a Man's Life*, op. cit., p. 209.

Chapter 12—The Returning Question

1. Werner Kelber, *Mark's Story of Jesus, op. cit.*, p. 48.
2. Theodore Weeden, *Traditions in Conflict, op. cit.*, pp. 26–51. Also see Sean Kealy, *Mark's Gospel: A History of Its Interpretation, op. cit.*, pp. 193–195.
3. Theodore Weeden, *Traditions in Conflict, op. cit.*, p. 52.
4. *Ibid.*, pp. 52–53.
5. Wilfred Harrington, *Mark, op,. cit.*, p. 162.
6. Ernest Becker, *Denial of Death*, Macmillian: New York, 1975, pp. 197f.
7. These are segments taken from a series of poems writen between 1970 and 1973. They were duplicated for private distribution under the following titles: "Like Man Waiting," "Shout It Louder," "Search for an Answer" and "Birthing Once Again." They were basically a reflection on each of the four gospels. A new series of six poems dealing in part with the same question of life, death, and meaning have been gathered together in a booklet entitled *Whisperings of Many* and form the basis for a series of television programs entitled "Innervision" produced by Telicare, Diocesan Television Center, Uniondale, New York. An explanation of the approach and thought of the poems together with an analysis of the poems themselves is provided by Peter Mann in *Innervision: Journey into the Image: A Study Guide*, Diocesan Television Center, 1345 Admiral Lane, Uniondale, N.Y. 11553.
8. "Now the victory of the Creator and Redeemer in the Christian vision is to have transformed what is in itself a universal power of diminishment and extinction into an essentially life-giving factor. God must in some way or other make room for himself, hollowing us out and emptying us if he is finally to penetrate into us. And in order to assimilate us in him he must break down the molecules of our being so as to recast and remodel us. The function of death is to provide the necessary entrance into our innermost selves": Teilhard de Chardin, *Le Milieu Divin, op. cit.*, p. 61.

9. Elisabeth Kübler-Ross, *On Death and Dying:* Macmillian: New York, 1975; *Death: The Final Stage of Growth*, Prentice-Hall, Englewood Cliffs, 1975.

10. Peter Kreeft's study is philosophical in orientation and less well known than that of Kübler-Ross. Death, he suggests, conceals a great secret behind its appearance like the human face (p. 9). He then describes the five faces as : 1. The Enemy, 2. The Stranger, 3. The Friend, 4. The Mother, 5. The Lover: Peter S. Kreeft, *Love Is Stronger Than Death*, Harper and Row: San Francisco, 1979.

11. Mayer's study is a more "popular" than scientific study. This makes for easy reading and ready absorption. I call her work descriptive as opposed to the more original and technical works mentioned above. She says there are traditionally three phases to the rites of passage in mid-life: 1. social disengagement and psychological dying, 2. a time and a place of isolation outside familiar boundaries, and 3. psychological rebirth and social reintegration. Among other things she advises us to 1. take the mid-life crisis seriously, 2. recognize the need to mourn, 3. take responsibility for your own life, 4. re-examine your values and goals, 5. learn to substitute new sources of gratification for old, 6. get in touch with your feelings, 7. respect your body, 8. discontinue polyphasic thinking, 9. listen without interrupting, 10. have a retreat in your home: Nancy Mayer, *The Male Mid-Life Crisis: Fresh Starts After Forty*, Doubleday: New York, 1978, pp. 246–252.

12. Michael Novak, *The Experience of Nothingness*, Harper: New York, 1970, p. 115.

13. Peter S. Kreeft, *Love Is Stronger Than Death, op. cit.*, p. 31.

Chapter 13—The Transfiguration

1. Theodore Weeden, *Traditions in Conflict, op. cit.*, pp. 118–124.

2. Eduard Schweizer, *The Good News According to Mark, op. cit.*, pp. 180–186.

3. Rosemary Haughton, *The Passionate God*, Paulist Press: New York, 1981, p. 67.

4. Werner Kelber, *Mark's Story of Jesus, op. cit.*, p. 53.

5. Rosemary Haughton, *The Passionate God, op. cit.*, p. 66: "The story of the transfiguration is in the middle in the obvious sense that chronologically the three Synoptic Gospels put it about midway in the public life of Jesus, not in terms of length of time (we cannot know precisely the actual time involved anyway) but in the sense that it formed a kind of watershed in the career of Jesus . . . and it is in the middle in the sense that it takes place not in one sphere or another but across the boundaries releasing one into another in the oddest way."

6. John Sheets, S. J., *The Spirit Speaks in Us*, Dimension Books: Denville, 1969, p. 25.

7. Rosemary Haughton, *The Passionate God, op. cit.*, pp. 83f.

8. James Plastaras, C. M., *The God of Exodus*, Bruce: Milwaukee, 1966, pp. 202–258, 316–318.

9. Mt 4:1f; Mk 1:12–13; Lk 4:1–13.

10. Mt 5–7; Lk 6:20.

11. Jn 6; Mt 14:13; Mk 6:30; Lk 9:10.

12. Lk 22:35; Mt 26:36; Mk 14:32.

13. Lk 22:23; Mk 15:21f; Jn 19:17f.

14. Lk 24:5.

15. Mk 9; Lk 9; Mt 17.

16. D. E. Nineham, *Saint Mark, op. cit.*, p. 234.

17. Wilfred Harrington, *Mark, op. cit.*, p. 136.

18. *Ibid.*

19. *Ibid.*

20. William Kraft, *Search for the Holy*, Fortress: Philadelphia, 1971, p. 106.

21. Rosemary Haughton, *The Passionate God, op. cit.*, p. 79.

22. Kieran Kavanagh and Otilio Rodriquez, trans., *The Collected Works of St. John of the Cross*, Institute of Carmelite Studies, Washington, D.C., 1973. Cf. especially the commentary on Book 2, pp. 107–212. In addition one could read a very excellent and readable description of a person going through the

stages of conversion as described by John of the Cross in Thomas S. Kane's article "Gentleness in John of the Cross," *Contemplative Review*, Winter 1981, Vol. 14, No. 4: Spring 1982, Vol. 15, No. 1; Summer 1982, Vol. 15, No. 2: Barre, Vermont.

23. Kieran Kavanagh and Otilio Rodriquez, trans., *The Collected Works of St. John of the Cross, op. cit.*, p. 315.

24. Elizabeth Boyden Howes, *Man the Choicemaker*, Westminster, 1973. The quotation here is from Dorothy B. Phillips, Elizabeth B. Howes, Lucille M. Nixon, *The Choice Is Always Ours: An Anthology of the Religious Way*, Theosophical Publishing House: Wheaton, 1975, p. 208.

Chapter 14—The Temple

1. David Rhoads and Donald Michie, *Mark as Story, op. cit.*, p. 70.

2. Werner Kelber, *Mark's Story of Jesus, op. cit.*, pp. 58–59.

3. Fulton J. Sheen, *Life of Christ*, Doubleday: Garden City, 1977, p. 260.

4. Joseph Wortman, "The Mother Image: Three New Testament Symbols," *Contemplative Review*, Summer 1977, pp. 16–24.

5. Jacques Jiminez and Daniel O'Connor, *The Images of Jesus*, Winston Press: Minneapolis, 1977, pp. 136f. These authors are primarily concerned with the Matthean account and they set out to see if they study Jesus' attempt to come to terms with the leading metaphor of the world into which he was born. They find that as Jesus confronts the received metaphor of temple he exhibited the four attitudes we have recorded. I have felt free to translate that observation to apply to Mark's Gospel.

6. Hamish Swanston, *The Community Witness*, Sheed and Ward: New York, 1967.

7. *Ibid.*, pp. 125–130.

8. Pierre Teilhard de Chardin, *Hymn of the Universe*, Harper and Row: New York, 1969, p. 79.

9. Ernest Becker, *Escape from Evil,* Macmillan: New York, 1976, p. 81. Becker quotes freely from, and acknowledges his own indebtedness to, Rank, Hocart and Brown. I therefore include here his references to their works: Norman O. Brown, *Life Against Death: The Psychoanalytical Meaning of History,* New York: Harper and Row, 1954; A. M. Hocart, *The Life-Giving Myth,* London: Methuen, 1952; Otto Rank, *Beyond Psychology,* Dover Books: New York, 1958.

10. *Ibid.,* p. 81.

11. Helen M. Luke, *Woman, Earth and Spirit: The Feminine in Symbol and Myth,* Crossroad: New York, 1981, pp. 79–93.

Chapter 15—The Third Day

1. Cf. Chapter 5 above.

2. Cf. Howard C. Kee and Franklin W. Young, *The Living World of the New Testament,* Darton, Longman and Todd: London, 1962, p. 49, for a discussion of the difference.

3. Regis Duffy, *Real Presence, Worship, Sacraments and Commitment,* Harper and Row: San Francisco, 1982, p. 66.

4. Erik Erikson, *Childhood and Society,* W. W. Norton: New York, 1978, pp. 270–271.

5. Carl Gustav Jung, *Memories, Dreams, Reflections,* ed. Aniela Jaffe, trans. Richard and Clare Winston, Random House: New York, 1963, p. 325.

6. Eduard Schweizer, *The Good News According to Mark, op. cit.,* p. 237.

7. *Ibid.,* p. 238.

8. Arland Hultgren, *Jesus and His Adversaries,* Augsburg: Minneapolis, 1979, pp. 68f.

9. Paul Tournier, *A Place for You,* Harper and Row: New York, 1968, p. 159.

10. Pierre Teilhard de Chardin, "Reflections on Happiness," in *Toward the Future,* Harcourt Brace Jovanovich: New York, 1975, pp. 107–129. There is no substitute for the writing of Teilhard himself in his original works, especially: *Christianity and Evolution,* Harcourt Brace Jovanovich, 1971; *Hymn of the*

Universe, Harper and Row, 1975; *Human Energy*, Harcourt Brace Jovanovich, 1969; *The Future of Man*, Harper and Row, 1964; *Science and Christ*, Harper and Row, 1968; *The Divine Milieu*, Harper and Row, 1960; *The Phenomenon of Man*, Harper and Row, 1965.

11. Viktor Frankl, *Psychotherapy and Existentialism: Selected Papers on Logotherapy, op. cit.*, p. 12.

12. Eduard Schweizer, *The Good News According to Mark, op. cit.*, p. 245.

13. Arland Hultgren, *Jesus and His Adversaries, op. cit.*, pp. 122–131.

14. Wilfred Harrington, *Mark*, op. cit., p. 188.

15. John Donahue, "Jesus as the Parable of God in the Gospel of Mark," in James Luther Mays, *Interpreting the Gospels*, Fortress Press: Philadelphia, 1981, pp. 162–163.

16. Carlo Carretto, *The God Who Comes*, Maryknoll: New York, 1976, p. 23.

17. John Dunne has richly explored this theme in his writing: *Time and Myth*, S. C. M.: London, 1973; *The Way of All the Earth*, Macmillan: New York, 1972; *City of the Gods*, Macmillan: New York, 1973.

18. Eduard Schweizer, *The Good News According to Mark, op. cit.*, p. 253.

19. John S. Dunne, *Time and Myth: A Meditation on Storytelling as an Exploration of Life and Death*, S. C. M.: London, 1979, p. 113.

20. Thomas Berry, "The New Story," in *Riverdale Papers V*, Riverdale Center for Religious Research, Riverdale, New York 10471.

21. Arland Hultgren, *Jesus and His Adversaries, op. cit.*, pp. 45–47.

22. Paul Achtemeier, "Mark as Interpreter of the Jesus Tradition," in James Luther Mays, *Interpreting the Gospels, op. cit.*, p. 127.

23. Eduard Schweizer, *The Good News According to Mark, op. cit.*, p. 266.

24. Thomas Mann, *Death in Venice—Stories of Three Decades*, Alfred Knopf: New York, 1976, p. 395.

25. For further information on this matter, cf. Phillip Howes Nixon, ed., *The Choice Is Always Ours*, Request Books: Illinois, 1975; Evelyn Underhill, *Mysticism*, E. P. Dutton: New York, 1961; H. A. Remhold, ed., *The Soul Afire*, Doubleday: New York, 1973; Herbert Weiner, *Nine and One Half Mystics—The Kabbala Today*, Macmillan: New York, 1976.

Chapter 16—Absence and Presence

1. Werner Kelber, *The Passion in Mark, op. cit.*, p. 173.
2. Eduard Schweizer, *The Good News According to Mark, op. cit.*, p. 296.
3. Werner Kelber, *Mark's Story of Jesus, op. cit.*, p. 72.
4. Eduard Schweizer, *The Good News According to Mark, op. cit.*, p. 365.
5. Francoise Dolto and Gerard Severin, *The Jesus of Psychoanalysis: A Freudian Interpretation of the Gospel*, Doubleday: New York, 1979, p. 141.
6. Henri Nouwen, *Reaching Out: The Three Movements of the Spiritual Life*, Doubleday: New York, 1975, p. 91.
7. Walter Burghardt, S. J., *Seasons That Laugh Or Weep*, Paulist Press: New York, 1983, pp. 101–102.
8. Eduard Schweizer, *The Good News According to Mark, op. cit.*, p. 295; Werner Kelber, *Mark's Story of Jesus, op. cit.*, p. 74.

9.

11:1–6	14:13–16
v1 He sent two of his disciples	v13 He sent two of his disciples
v2 and said to them Go into the village . . . and . . . you will find	and said to them Go into the city . . . and . . . will meet you.
v3 Say "The Lord. . . .	v14 Say . . . The Teacher
v4 And they went away and they found	v16 And they went out . . . and found
v6 as Jesus had said and	as he had told them and. . . .

Vernon Robbins, "Last Meal: Preparation, Betrayal, and Absence," in Werner Kelber, *The Passion in Mark, op. cit.,* p. 23.

10. *Ibid.,* p.35.
11. *Ibid.,* p. 38.
12. *Ibid.,* p. 35.
13. Rosemary Haughton, *The Passionate God, op. cit.,* p. 182.
14. Henri Nouwen, *Out of Solitude,* Ave Maria Press: Notre Dame, 1975, p. 61.

Chapter 17—Gethsemani

1. Werner Kelber, ed., *The Passion in Mark, op. cit.,* pp. 47–50.
2. David Rhoads and Donald Michie, *Mark as Story, op. cit.,* p. 54.
3. Werner Kelber, *Mark's Story of Jesus, op. cit.,* p. 76.
4. David Stanley, in *Jesus in Gethsemani,* Paulist Press: New York, 1979, pp. 128–151, calls Gethsemani a "school of prayer."
5. Matthew dots the i's; what was already intelligible in Mark becomes even more so in Matthew who contrasts "here" with "over there." Cf. Pierre Benoit, *The Passion and Resurrection of Jesus Christ,* Herder and Herder: New York, 1970, p. 14.

Chapter 18—The Passion

1. James Luther Mays, *Interpreting the Gospels, op. cit.,* p. 130.
2. Werner Kelber, ed., *The Passion in Mark, op. cit.,* pp. 172–176. One should also consult David Rhoads and Donald Michie, *Mark as Story, op. cit.,* pp. 101–136. They devoted a considerable amount of space to the concept of characters in the Gospel.
3. George T. Montague, S. M., *Mark, Good News for Hard Times, op. cit.,* p. 179.
4. Edward J. Mally suggests that this division is an artificial construction that reflects a liturgical ambiance. Cf. "Commentary on Mark," *Jerome Biblical Commentary,* Prentice-Hall: Englewood Cliffs, 1968, Vol. II, p. 58.

5. Pierre Benoit, *Jesus and the Gospel,* Herder and Herder, 1973, pp. 123f.; also Pierre Benoit, *The Passion and Resurrection of Jesus Christ, op. cit.,* pp. 79f.
6. Pierre Benoit, *The Passion and Resurrection of Jesus Christ, op. cit.,* p. 136.
7. George T. Montague, *Mark, Good News For Hard Times, op. cit.,* p. 178.
8. Virginia Satir suggests that there are four universal patterns of response people use to get around the threat of rejection. In each case the responder is seeking to conceal his weakness. She lists them as Placating, Blaming, Computing and Distracting. A fifth response she calls Leveling or Flowing; it is, she believes, the only one that really works. It alone has the chance to heal ruptures, break impasses, or build bridges between people. It is this contrast I have in mind between Pilate's placating stance and Jesus' leveling one. One could use Satir's framework to elaborate on the other characters also and see how the whole passion opens us up to our system of communication.Cf. Virginia Satir, *Peoplemaking,* Science and Behavior Books: Palo Alto, 1972, pp. 58–80.
9. George T. Montague, *Mark, Good News for Hard Times, op. cit.,* p. 184.
10. James Carroll, *The Winter Name of God,* Sheed and Ward: New York, 1975, p. 168.
11. Anthony Storr, *The Integrity of Personality,* Atheneum: New York, 1961, pp. 41–43.

Chapter 19—Passion

1. Matthew Fox, *Breakthrough: Meister Eckhart's Creation Spirituality in New Translation,* Doubleday: New York, 1980; Raymond Blakney, trans., *Meister Eckhart,* Harper and Row: New York, 1941. This latter work includes works not translated in Matthew Fox and especially Eckhart's defense against charges of heresy.

2. Matthew Fox, *Breakthrough: Meister Eckhart's Creation Spirituality in New Translation, op. cit.,* p. 169.

3. Sebastian Moore, *The Fire and the Rose Are One,* Seabury: New York, 1980, pp. 144–145.

4. Thomas Merton, *Seasons of Celebration,* Farrar, Strauss, Giroux: New York, 1980, pp. 204–215.

5. Sam Keen, *Beginnings Without End,* Harper and Row: New York, 1975, p. 70.

6. Karl Rahner, "Thomas Aquinas on the Incomprehensibility of God," in *Celebrating the Medieval Heritage: A Colloquy on the Thought of Aquinas and Bonaventure, Journal of Religion* 58, Supplement, 1978. The quote here is that printed in Robert M. Doran, "Jungian Psychology and Christian Spirituality III," *Review for Religious,* Vol. 38, No. 6, November 1979, p. 858.

7. Teilhard de Chardin, *The Divine Milieu, op. cit.,* pp. 89–90. Cf. also the great statement in the prayer *Hymn of the Universe:* "In death we are caught up, overwhelmed, dominated by that divine power which lies within the forces of inner disintegration and, above all, within that irresistible yearning which will drive the separated soul on to complete its farther, predestined journey as infallibly as the sun causes the mists to rise from the water on which it shines. Death surrenders us completely to God; it makes us pass into God. In return we have to surrender ourselves to it, in love and in the abandon of love, since, when death comes to us, there is nothing further for us to do but let ourselves be entirely dominated and led onwards by God": *Hymn of the Universe,* Harper: New York, 1969, p. 150.

Chapter 20—Beyond an Empty Tomb

1. Edward Schillebeeckx, *Jesus, op. cit.,* p. 343.

2. Pierre Benoit, *Passion and Resurrection, op. cit.,* p. 247.

3. Edward Schillebeeckx, *Jesus, op. cit.,* p. 335.

4. *Ibid.* p. 336.
5. Raymond Brown, *The Virginal Conception and Bodily Resurrection of Jesus*, Paulist Press: New York, 1973, pp. 69f.
6. Teilhard de Chardin, *Human Energy*, Harcourt Brace Jovanovich: New York, 1969, pp. 63f.
7. John Sanford, *Fritz Kunkel: Selected Writings*, Paulist Press: New York, 1984, pp. 364–375.